SpringerBriefs in Law

More information about this series at http://www.springer.com/series/10164

Jan M. Broekman · Frank Fleerackers

Legal Signs Fascinate

Kevelson's Research on Semiotics

Springer

Jan M. Broekman
Faculty of Law
KU Leuven
Leuven
Belgium

and

Penn State Law
Penn State University
University Park, PA
USA

Frank Fleerackers
Faculty of Law
KU Leuven
Leuven
Belgium

ISSN 2192-855X ISSN 2192-8568 (electronic)
SpringerBriefs in Law
ISBN 978-3-319-69519-8 ISBN 978-3-319-69520-4 (eBook)
https://doi.org/10.1007/978-3-319-69520-4

Library of Congress Control Number: 2017955647

Printed on acid-free paper

This Springer imprint is published by Springer Nature
The registered company is Springer International Publishing AG
The registered company address is: Gewerbestrasse 11, 6330 Cham, Switzerland

Contents

Introduction

This Brief underlines most forcefully that this century's fascination by signs, signals, shortcuts, and related components of the globally spread e-language is one of its eye-catching features. That was not imaginable at the end of the twentieth century, and Roberta Kevelson (1931–1998) who introduced the term 'legal semiotics' since her 1977 publication *Inlaws/Outlaws: A Semiotics of Systematic Interaction* could not foresee that change. But such observation is in itself already a motivation for further research in Kevelson's work. The impact of the turn in law and legal theory she propagated remained in the dark since her death in 1998 during decades.

Today, lawyers illustrate the reverse: Law does not have any effect if it is without the fascination for signs and their function of signifying. We need to raise questions again, such as: Who was at the origins and first effects of the concept 'legal semiotics' within legal discourse? Today that still seems a non-issue. Yet it appears necessary to recover that occurrence, because it is incorporated in a scholar, which was on the one hand influenced by the very first feminist movements at the East coast of the USA and on the other hand by the philosophy of Charles Sanders Peirce and the semiotics of Thomas Sebeok. The two played until her days a minor role in legal theory and hermeneutics as well as the unfolding of understanding legal speech acts. Although the person in question, Roberta Kevelson, did not officially belong to the editors of the Journal, she was honored with a full issue of the *International Journal for the Semiotics of Law* less than a year after she passed away in 1998—the Journal she had so feverishly supported during the last decade of her career at Penn State University.

The Office Papers and Notes she left behind at the Reading Campus of the University were send to Texas Tech University (School of Law, Lubbock, TX) but remained unattended until 2008/2009. They should have played a role in the Penn State University Dickinson School of Law seminars: the *Roberta Kevelson Seminars of Law and Semiotics*,[1] which were on the program from 2008–2013.

[1]Broekman and Pencak (2009, 2010).

After the renewals of Law Programs, interest for the seminars faded away, accompanied by a growing disinterest for legal theoretical issues. This *Brief in Law* tries to contribute to a renewed interest for, and understanding of the many Kevelson attempts to bring law and semiotics together in an operative manner and on the basis of thoroughly reconsidered philosophical principles and ideas, honoring at the same time her hitherto unknown Office Papers and Notes that could fortify the bridges between law practices and legal theoretical implications.

References

Broekman JM, Pencak WA (2009) Lawyers making meaning. the Roberta Kevelson seminar on law and semiotics at Penn State University's Dickinson School of Law. Int J Semiot Law 22(1)

Broekman JM, Pencak WA (2010) Signs of law. the Roberta Kevelson seminar on law and semiotics at Penn State University's Dickinson School of Law. Int J Semiot Law 23(1)

Part I
Why

Chapter 1
Why's of Fascination

Abstract Modern times show a deeply rooted fascination for signs. Philosophers like Charles Sanders Peirce already registered that change of mind at the edge of the 20th century. He inspired Roberta Kevelson in her design of a *method* of knowledge seeking and questioning. She applied in that method many 'How's of 'Why' and 'Why's of 'How' in Law and the Legal Sciences. It formed the basis for unfolding the concept of *legal semiotics*. The latter highlighted new insights on signs in legal practice and in legal education.

Keywords Semiotics · Signs · Legal theory · Communication · Continuity

1.1 Peirce's Smile

We may regret that smart phones and social media did not exist in the days of the great US philosopher Charles Sanders Peirce (1839–1914). Had it been the case, we would today have been inspired by wonderful tweets like: "the universe is perfused with signs" or perhaps: "a thing without oppositions *ipso facto* does not exist"—and what would happen when our smart phone tells us repeatedly that "facts can only exist in relation(s)"? Such messages would not reach us as conclusions of scientific research or as the summary of lifelong cherished philosophical insights. They rather invite us to experience a particular *sphere* of life. Does the tweet: "my language is the sum total of my life" threaten us? 'A wonderful awakening'—Peirce would write with a smile. He likes his smart phone: not because of his own tweets but because it was so weird that such a small machine made the world so translucent. And it did so in an easy way. "To be liked, it is only necessary to be translucent", he wrote August 1860—leaving undecided whether it was his person or his phone! Do we know that difference today? Look around on the streets, in the train or autobus. Isn't it our self-portrait in the days of selfies?

J.M. Broekman and F. Fleerackers, *Legal Signs Fascinate*, SpringerBriefs in Law,
https://doi.org/10.1007/978-3-319-69520-4_1

1.2 Three Ladies, (1) and (2)

In October 1860 Peirce had closed a secret marriage contract; first unfolded in spoken words and later developed in writing. And it is well documented that he later married Harriet Melusina (or Zina) Fay, and then Juliette Pourtalais b. Froissy. Kenneth Ketner played with such data, and his wife completed that play with her observation on Peirce that "everything in life seemed to appear to him as an inquiry". Many letters of the subsequent marriages were safeguarded and they read today as if he conducted "some kind of psychology experiment to learn more about himself, especially about his developing powers of manipulating and controlling women… It appears beyond doubt that it was at least a part of what he called his study of the physiology of marriage. This idea seems even more plausible because he placed the file next to those passages from his private journal on lust and on witchcraft… and those words are clearly advice about mastering the *science* of seduction" she remarked. Her husband observed in his turn that she "might be right about that," and that Peirce could be classified "alongside other men of genius who exhibited a similar trait."[1] However, those three ladies were by no means the only ones to play a role in Peirce's thoughts.

Our attention is *mirabile dictu* also directed towards three other ladies in Peirce's life: they are his contemporaries: Lady Victoria Welby, his company for years after his death: Roberta Kevelson, and the Goddess of fate and semiotics: during the Greek 5th BC called Tyche, later alive as the Roman Goddess Fortuna. The three have been inseparable wherever the work of Peirce was and is mentioned. Lady Victoria Welby profiled Peirce through her correspondence and her initiative to promote *significs* as predecessor of modern semiotics. Roberta Kevelson did the same during her promotion and exploration of *legal* semiotics by means of her own writing in which Peirce was constantly present. And Tyche was for Peirce the omnipresent Goddess of semiotics and of the philosophical connections between *signs* and the *course of life* of every human being: the *synechism* resulting in the connectedness of things. That was all embracing for Peirce as well as Lady Welby, because it supported the doctrine that absolute chance plays definitively a role in the universe in guaranteeing *synechism*, the doctrine of *continuity* being the articulation of ultimate *togetherness* of all composites in the cosmos.[2]

1.3 Roberta Kevelson

We focus on Kevelson, her ideas and her work as a subject for further research. Much of her work and a majority of its contextual components offer the same sense about future research, of which law and social sciences may profit. We take notice

---

[1]Ketner (1988).

[2]Hardwick and Cook (1977), Schmitz (1990), Broekman and Backer (2015), Broekman (2011), Broekman (2013), Brent (1993).

of her biographic outlines, which combine important contributions to the early feminist movement at the US East Coast in the 60s and 70s with an outstanding and internationally recognized academic career in the 80s and 90s of the last century. This will be paralleled by bibliographical research and the establishing of a newly revised complete bibliography, as well as suggestions concerning further research into legal semiotics on the basis of the earlier mentioned papers and notes that were left in her office and were disregarded since.

In 1986 Roberta Kevelson published an article full of thoughts that encircled Peirce's ideas on 'Method', entitled: "How's of Why and Why's of How" (1986) and originally written for a conference on knowledge seeking and questioning. Her essay focused primarily on matters of rhetoric and semiotics: manners of speech and manners of meaning making. Those components are in surprising proximity to the daily work of the modern lawyer with its "why's and how's" that are questions of his or her client as well as motivations mirroring those questions in herself.

There are several reasons why law and legal discourse are widely and deeply accepted in modern society. All this seems a justification for this Briefs title. Acceptance of law is only seldom the result of a personal appreciation, but most generally are institutional powers contouring individual and social structures in an acceptable manner. A group of those issues is based on the strength of the interrelations between the social effects of law on the one hand and politics on the other. Another set of issues is founded on the fact, that interactivity is appreciated as a completion of human existence in general, so that law is able to contribute essentially to the fulfillment of human destiny. Both justify a fascinating observation: although the question 'what is law' may not be a matter of common *knowledge*, it is decidedly a matter of essence in the *realization* of human life. If law fascinates, it does so as a precious component of the latter.

1.4 Sign and Signs

Daily life appears to be a 'sign pool' to all of us: not only to the police officer or to the teacher is confronted with this feeling but we all experience that sign pool as essential for us. Each individual is confronted with signs as a deep form of otherness the world has put around us. That mysterious component, which we name 'sign' and want to read as well as interpret has been explained by the US philosopher Charles Sanders Peirce as the result of the fact that *everything can become a sign*. Living is pooling in the immersion of signs. Social manners, ethical guidelines, grammatical indications, legal commands and social instructions, fixated fragments of knowledge form a forthwith variety of signs, which we call reality. The wealth of that variety is not only shocking but also fascinating. If law fascinates, it is because law is part of that variety—a variety that challenges legal imagination beyond limits. Ask modern cosmologists and quote the sentence, the 'tweet' of Peirce, which tells them that 'the universe is perfused with signs'. They answer with the statement, that the universe itself is also a sign in the midst of universes, which we will never perceive and about which our knowledge will shipwreck. So, we have to tell subjects of law as well as lawyers, that signs are of essence for law and its manifold discourses.

An insight loaded with consequences for the exercise of all sorts of legal practice is, that *communication* appears a vital component of each activity a lawyer brings to the fore. Lawyers and philosophers in the course of centuries of thought formation in the Occident have recognized this power of communication as an inherent force of law. It was communication among citizens that colored the upper part of Hobbes' illustration; it was the preference for specific sets of communication that dictated Solon to design laws and law-like remarks about society; it was the power of governance that inspired and enforced Napoleon to formulate his Civil Code. Fascination caused by law is most often a fascination for the power to mould forms of communication. And it is in this perspective most important to formulate that there is no communication without signs. Message creation and messaging itself depend on signs and sign systems. All social institutions created their particular sign systems, and law's top position does not surprise.

There are at least two applications of this insight that explore the internal power of law and communication in relation to signs and sign systems: (a) legal education is one of the most important among them—training in legal thought formation and legal communication patterns includes an in-depth understanding of signs and their fascinating contexts (no matter whether they are traffic signs or signs constructing penal law, tax laws or corporate laws). (b) Activist attitudes of lawyers, which explore critical social situations and want to provoke social change in key regions of society focus in the performance of their speech activity on the sign character of situations in which they as well as the segments of the population they care for, are involved. Signs in law educate and are exquisite materials for legal education programs, not in the least because signs in law make it possible to envisage social change.

1.5 Legal Semiotics Fascinates

Those observations underline the importance of legal semiotics as a prevailing legal theory in the second decade of this century. To understand law as a system of signs, all philosophical presuppositions included, fits to the developments of electronic communication. It fits to the many forms of tweets and twitters and their smart phones on the street, to electronic traffic regulations on streets, in harbors and their ships, to planes around and on our airports—as well as the support of medical interventions in modern automated surgery rooms. Communication differs fundamentally from its meanings in the second decade of the past century. Modern law and its fascination is this decade's product; both share the mentioned difference. Two aspects appear: (a) the importance of legal semiotics as the predominant form of legal theory unfolds in this decade, (b) a central question of that dominance is, whether a legal theory can be synthetic (fitting to the semiotic approach) and not overall analytic, as was the case in earlier centuries.

The fascination law awakens for its techniques and purposes in the minds of citizens and lawyers alike is not only a matter of legal practice or of the many ways law exhibits itself in society, embracing vaguely also legal scholars. Such a fascination was noticed in the effects the German Historic School created in Germany, and above all the response the School's thoughts encountered in the Russian legal world. Many Russian law professors and higher judges were sent out to Berlin in order to study and re-orientate themselves in the legal sciences of the day. The history of the American Founding Fathers and the related manifestations in Philadelphia could also be described as specific forms of fascination for legal thoughts and thinking, which were ultimately laid down in the texts of the American Constitution, its Preamble and Amendments. Of course, there were political forces and considerations involved, and political goals to be achieved. But all in all, one can observe that legal history in the Occident encountered many phases of enthusiasm and fascination, which were seldom reflected in legal theory but remained restricted to citizen reactions in public. The history of legal concepts seems separated from the history of their public appreciation or depreciation. To inverse the directions of that tendency seems inherent to any development of legal semiotics.

A lawyer pleading before a Court to be allowed and being able to 'say for law' touches in this plead the most important fragments of social life. She was in the position to ask a group of functionaries a permission to qualify the issue(s) at hand in a particular manner: the legal manner. At the same time she asked to work from now on with the words 'said for law' in all structures of representation she meets. Those structures reach from her client in particular to society in general. That position, including the meanings involved and the signs being allowed to carry, is deeply social by its nature. No wonder, that legal semiotics is preferred as a pillar of legal education.

References

Brent J (1993) Charles Sanders Peirce: a life, Indiana UP, Bloomington & Indianapolis, p 69f

Broekman JM (2011) A goddess for semiotics of law and legal discourse, DADA–Rivista Di Antropologia Post-Globale. In: Palmisano A (ed) Trieste

Broekman JM (2013) Artificiality and naturalness–The Tyche Deity. In: Broekman JM, Backer CL (eds) Lawyers making meaning, Springer, Dordrecht, p 217ff

Broekman JM, Backer CL (2015) (eds) Signs in law—a source book, Springer, Heidelberg, p 89ff

Hardwick S, Cook J (eds) (1977) Semiotics and significs. The Correspondence Between Charles S. Peirce and Victoria Lady Welby, Indiana UP, Bloomington

Ketner KL (1988) His glassy essence. An Autobiography of Charles Sanders Peirce. Vanderbilt UP, Nashville, London, p 213f

Schmitz WH (1990) Essays on significs. Papers Presented on the Occasion of the 150th Anniversary of the Birth of Lady Welby, J. Benjamins, Amsterdam/Philadelphia

Chapter 2
Social Life and Law

Abstract Social life is life spoken. Speech acts appear of central importance in studying law, as semiotics underline. Law is multidimensional, lawyers speak everyday language *and* legal language and the meaning of their words is seldom restricted to one level of significance. Is Law's *discourse* a different manifestation of linguistic expressiveness? Signs in law reinforce and enrich social life while introducing new dimensions of meaning. This was Greimas' important contribution to semiotics, as we understand. It was also the reason why Lyotard unfolded his theory of narratives, once confronted with law in post-modernity. Those insights in what Kevelson named the n-dimensionality of meaning and significance in life widens the forces of freedom to create commonness.

Keyword Speech-act · Discourse · Freedom · Meaning · Narration Post-modernity

2.1 Social Life

There is no social life without language—no matter what stadium of development a language has reached and no matter whether that language is mainly determined by verbal or by non-verbal articulations. All components of a humanly understood and experienced world are named by means of a language. All activities of humans are qualified by means of names. Those processes create a fundamental *freedom* to understand and act, a freedom to explore life in all its dimensions. The example of the lawyer asking the Court 'to say for law' includes a particular social structure with its predominant level of linguistic expressiveness, which we generally call 'institutional' in the case of law. Such features do *not* relate to the particular language that determines the specific profession in the first place, but to the social structure we qualify as 'legal'. As law students or as lawyers we have to recognize that we belong to that institution. It says *firstly*, that the lawyer asking the Court is and should be *a lawyer like all others*. There is no exception on that rule, and the language in effect before the Court has in that regard only one type of speaker.

J.M. Broekman and F. Fleerackers, *Legal Signs Fascinate*, SpringerBriefs in Law,
https://doi.org/10.1007/978-3-319-69520-4_2

Secondly, the meaning of 'saying/being said for law' is *not* in the hands of the lawyer or of judges speaking, but more generally in the hands of *others*—possibly also non-lawyers, such as members of a Jury, politicians or specialists in a particular discipline. This indicates that *legal signs refer to a diversity of social meanings* and interpretations of meaning. Lawyers speak as if they utter a natural language but their application of those language suggest at least a parallel realm of meaning, which concerns the law as an institution specifically.

This parallel between natural language and artificial language and the exploration of one in the other has been understood by philosophers of language in the 20th century, such as Russell and Wittgenstein, as well as specialists in research on meaning such as Lady Victoria Welby (1903), De Haan (1916), Ogden and Richards (1923) or Ch. Morris (1946). Their approach to language was in many regards also a philosophy of law and legal discourse. Their interest concerned the foundational dimensions of a lawyer's activity, with priority given to their specific management of meaning—which includes legal semiotics.

How can one explain the ties between fascination created by law and fascination caused by our perception of signs, which actually function in social life? The question seems overwhelming, new, unanswerable and a task too heavy and elaborate for a legal researcher in any legal system. Yet, the question touches one of the pillars of the actual views in law, which are in speech, in signs and in signification—and: what is more: on the path from sign to significance, in other words: in the semiotics of law. Our considerations should not destroy that fascination of law, which is truly a central social force!

2.2 Legal Discourse

Roberta Kevelson seldom mentioned the concept of a *discourse*, and certainly not of a *legal discourse.* One can only guess why she did not. It is evident that legal semiotics display a complex structure. One of the reasons could be that there is no definitive answer to the question "what is law" and that this lacking definition is in many regards an offense to the models and methods of thinking signs and semiosis. Law is a *process* and its speech acts, its many considerations about language, its uncertainties in text-interpretation and wider hermeneutic dimensions might make the discourse concept disappear from the frontlines and fit to articulations less than to facts, figures and truths. But in contrast, it seems that the latter and their *meaning* are still regarded as the more important legal component. Is law not mainly experienced as a norm, a value or an institutionally qualified set of expectations in social life?

Additional considerations are at stake. First there is the temptation to emphasize the *system*-character of law. That was clearer in the days of the first proposals about legal semiotics than it is to us today. With Friedman's 1975 *The Legal System* it appeared evident that legal semiotics has many ties with issues of systemic character. And this confirmed in itself the Peircean idea according to which a system is a continuum, a unified and cohesive pattern of signs constructed of sign relations. In a certain sense were properties of a discourse transferred to the system concept, particularly where Friedman's insight became accepted that law is only one of the many social systems, which give society a meaning. We thus have to keep in mind that the discursive character of legal articulations remains in proximity to what a system character forwarded.

These insights are not solely theoretical—they are immediately directed towards the reality that *social life is a speaking life*! Human lives in contemporary cultures are filled with speech acts and discourses. That may have been different in earlier times where hominids lived in closer and different relations with nature and in different patterns of relation among themselves, but today's life is marked by lingual utterances, which embrace verbal as well as non-verbal dimensions.[1] They appear to have properties that are far beyond strictly determined and precisely circumscribed goals. With the recognition of the latter returns the question pertaining to a more profiled understanding of the discourse concept.

A discourse is more evidently at distance to the large majority of utterances one encounters in ordinary life experiences than any systemic articulation. Our daily utterances often suggest such a system, but that is treacherous and simply incorrect. That incorrectness can, however, not be controlled because there are no methodical and sufficiently reliable data for any controlling performance. The idea itself, that our speech activity should be a performance of reliable 1:1 relations between reality and utterance, is a fairytale.

Everyday-language is a language on itself, a natural, non-artificial, non-professional language, which rather conceals meanings than uses well-determined meanings as building blocks for walls or cells called 'elementary particles'. What is expressed in natural language embraces various and often completely opposite meanings, paradoxes, impossibilities, mirages, pitfalls, jokes, choices, alternatives or fluid alterations without any hesitation. The concealment of meaning hides the enormous power of change and its dynamics, which is so effective in human articulation.

Peirce remarked that a natural language is an example for the study of semiotics in its entirety: the latter must from the very beginning relinquish any desire of having systems at work. Are we psychologically able to accept paradoxes and pitfalls without accompanying feelings of uncertainty? They are altogether *things said* and their property of being said makes them to an utterance, or what Foucault famously called 'enunciation'. That concerns any thought pattern focusing on *signs* and on *law* as an axial discourse in modern life. Do not forget in how many ways the two are tied together.

All human forms of communication need symbols and signs, and all human activities need meanings to become attached to those symbols and signs. Participating in a common discourse is a means of passing those signs and their meanings on from individual to individual—that's what we use to call 'culture'.

---

[1]Broekman (2017).

During this mostly concealed process, our attention has changed from the *content* of articulation (what was said) to the structure and essence of that *articulation itself* (how and under what condition it was said). Legal discourse has in this dynamic view a central role to play. Kevelson once remarked that "… the basic concepts of rights, resources, and reality take on new dimensions of meaning in correspondence with n-dimensional, infinite value judgments or truth-like beliefs which one holds."[2]

Her observation is correct for law, and it is correct for daily discourse. Both discourses are more than an ongoing talk, a simple conversation or an innocent report of feelings and thoughts about the world around us. What we say is never solely the registration of what is, and that is true in everyday life as well as in law. In life, a culture that formatted us is repeated, confirmed and stabilized with every articulation we exchange.

In law, a social power is repeated, confirmed and stabilized with concepts and values that lawyers prepare for our community in which we proliferate our culture. In doing so, lawyers experience the need to speak a discourse beyond their mother tongue. They thus experience that any meaning formation affects cultural dimensions, which form multiple layers of public life. In other words: laymen and lawyers experience their existence as 'being in the sign pool of today's culture.[3] Discourses tell us about our being in the sign pool, their collected utterances form an encyclopedia of the culture we all are while we convey its basic elements in all our speech activities.

2.3 Signs, Practice and Theory

The suggestion that a discourse should combine numerous fixed entities like small building blocks, and confirm stability prepared by samples of fixed properties, is tragically false. That idea just damages law's discourse, and while doing so it creates a deeply dysfunctional understanding of law in society—as happens often in critical times of the Occidental culture. The heart of this matter is, that neither law or society or culture evolves in a static mode. On the contrary: legal discourse moves continuously, and its creations are only valid for a specific period of time. The entire architecture of law's discourse is a matter of fluidity, of change, of anti-fixation, of incidental judgment and temporary insight as well as a matter of its own time-determination in the crossings of cultures. Law is like our culture: a *film*. Its discourse shows pictures, it mirrors values, it enlarges public opinions or scales them down, it stabilizes what changes too fast to function, it continuously refers to itself in the context of other discourses, it mirrors its culture and cultural ideals.

The consequence of that insight leads to a bewildering conclusion: *law's discourse is never alone* or unassailable in its being detached. On the contrary, it is

[2]Kevelson (1988), p. 7.

[3]Broekman (2016), p. 9ff, 193.

always in context; its contexts are most often specific social signs, no law is created outside of culture and the human mind. No legal regulation can exist or become effective as a single human articulation. Lawyers thus notice the relevance and the limits of their professional articulation when they are confronted with the unfolding of their own language: there is always a theory behind them and the requirements of a practice to follow obediently.

That situation is beyond doubt an emotional burden: for the practicing lawyer on the street as well as for the judge in Court. Each fragment of any engagement in law's discourse includes a confrontation with the major features of that discourse: the existence and powerful influence of encircling discourses, the specificities of a natural language in which features of law's discourse have to be communicated far beyond it's own limits, the fact that a legal discourse will always be evaluated according to its representation at the surface of its verbal (in particular textual) or non-verbal (in moments of violent behavior) appearances.

So there is an urgent need to remember the research of Greimas who combined his analysis of *sign* with the *discourse* and suggested, that each *text* has at least three levels of essence: a *surface* level, an *in-depth* level and a level of *representation.* This differentiation is a central issue in semiotics, which did not receive enough attention of social scientists, linguists or philosophers. It means, that not only a discourse, but also that a sign is never appropriately understood in the traditional speaker-hearer model. This insight is the consequence of the dynamic character of every lingual utterance or sign of a human individual. Greimas mentions:

- *deep structures*, which define the fundamental mode of existence of an individual or a society, and subsequently the conditions of existence of semiotic objects. As far as we know, the elementary constituents of deep structures have a definable logical status.
- *superficial structures* constitute a semiotics grammar system which arranges into discursive forms the contents susceptible of manifestation. The products of this grammar system are independent of the expression, which reveals them, in as far as they can theoretically appear in any substance, and, in the case of linguistic objects, in any language.
- *the structures of manifestation* produce and organize the significances."[4]

One should read this outline in relation with two important aspects:

(a) The *dynamic* character of all linguistic observations about human utterances is in effect within this pattern of development. Greimas suggested "that out of desire of intelligibility, we imagine that the human mind, in order to achieve the construction of a cultural object (literary, mythical, pictorial etc.) starts with simple elements and follows a complex course, encountering on its way constraints to which it must submit, as well as choices which it can make". It means that any author's view on the construction of a semiotics (sub)system goes hand in hand with elementary structures of meaning. From kernels of meaning to an exaltation of liberty unfolds the path from sign to signification.

[4]Greimas and Rastier (1968), 80f. Broekman and Backer (2015), p. 125ff.

(b) The *sign* as basic element of semiotics receives a *multidimensional meaning* through this observation. First, it is never alone. Second, it is present at most of the levels of lingual articulation, and third, it is just changing all the time in those various contexts. Fourth, Peirce was well aware of this dynamic variety of signs, when he differentiated between signs, sign-signs and other types, which were all present at various levels of texts, discourses and other layers of culture. Fifth, the riddle of those dynamics is for most semioticians (especially for those who study *legal* semiotics): when, how and where signs come to the surface and begin to unfold their representational (often institution-bound) life.

One should discern a particular feature: sign and discourse are both enveloped in an *unending dynamics* and therefore never caught and fixed forever, and they are both fundamentally *multi-layered* phenomena. Signs are, like discourses, in principle linked with other signs and discourses. The links between discourses are studied; Lyotard laid down their foundations in his theory about narratives and his insight that specific master–narratives format specific patterns of culture. A parallel theory about signs is not yet developed. The layered character of lingual utterances in which signs are evolved, the dynamics with surface and depth as their indications (signs) of limits, Greimas' metaphor of 'play' or Kevelson's 'film' are altogether issues of a future in-depth research program to understand legal semiotics in theory and its practices.

2.4 Semiotics, Linguistics and Language

Kevelson's ideas about the law being a system of signs do not touch the strong semiotic connections between *text* and *sign*. These ties focus especially in law on the traditional questions about interpretation and meaning of texts. But it is clear, that an understanding of texts does not lead to an equivalent understanding of signs. That insight forms a challenge in its own right. It is absolutely correct and generally understandable if one states that a sign needs a person or a subject that presents the sign and another subject that understands this presentation. That is the normal speaker–hearer model applied to the sign situation. It is sufficiently general and also quite understandable that a sign is in need of those two subjects, of which one fulfills the role of the sender and the other of the receiver. Can one understand a receiver without having a notion of a sender as its origin? One can decidedly *not*!

One remark should be clear and omnipresent: each understanding of a sign is like the understanding of an utterance. So, one asks: what is happening, when we articulate a word? What is the act of a speech act? What is its speech? Therefore: consider how proximate word and sign are in the framework of our discourse. Is that a new path to walk in linguistics whereby our daily notions of language play a hitherto unexplored role?

Let us go back to earlier observations. Peirce described in his 1873 manuscript *On the Nature of Signs* somewhat hesitatingly what we normally divide for the sake of our analysis in two parts. He wrote: (A) "…it is necessary for a sign to be a sign that it should be regarded as a sign for it is only a sign to that mind which so considers and if it is not a sign to any mind it is not a sign at all. It must be known to the mind first in its material qualities but also in its pure demonstrative application. That mind must conceive it to be connected with its object so that it is possible to reason from the sign to the thing". And (B) "Let us now see what the appeal of a sign to the mind amounts to. It produces a certain idea in the mind which is the idea that it is a sign of the thing it signifies and an idea is itself a sign, for an idea is an object and it represents an object."[5]

In (A) as well as in (B), there is the question of the mind as a conceiving instance. Semiotics is broadly understood as the science that deals with signs and the use of them by (mostly human) creatures, and that is an often too broadly conceived version of all human beings as sign-using creatures. Peirce refers not to such a definition of *a human being*, but to *the mind*—not considering whether other than human minds are forces that could be characterized as sign-related. Peirce's reference is to *a sign-related Self.* All that is sustained by his words, which focus on *relations*, not on fixed concepts regarding *beings*. And all that is a matter of the *mind of a Self.*

Here is again a subtle reference to the *dynamic* character, which embraces the sign. It puts the sign into a pattern of relations, because each element in the Cosmos should be understood in its interaction with and interdependence from every other element. Whenever the question arises whether man discovered the sign, the idea that signs belong to a humane evolution plays a role. The issue is, that a sign is not completely dependent on a sign-giver. The sign transcends any fixed relational patterns between sign-utterer and sign-receiver. Indeed, one could raise the question whether a sign can be uttered and received as if it were identical to a lingual utterance tat is marked by the infamous 'speaker–hearer' relationship. Hence the words in (B): the sign appeals to the mind, and produces the idea in the mind that it is a sign. That does *not* relate to an idealistic theory of knowledge, which regards the sign as the pure product of the mind.

The mind, Peirce suggests, is stimulated to produce the idea (that itself is a sign) that it conceives relations between itself and reality in terms of signs. *That occurrence does in modern Occidental culture primarily take place in texts and discourses.* Peirce's notes described what occurs in phenomena, which are characterized by their surface structure and their deep structures, whereby a level of representation plays a unique role. Indeed: a sign is only a sign when *it works*, i.e.: when it is a sign. The 'it works' is the sign of that sign-in-effect. Texts and discourses are two important regions in which we can observe signs-at-work. It does not mean that in other regions of human experience and culture signs do not work, but in those two they are most obvious. But: how? The answer is as simple as it is difficult: dynamically. That is, through being involved in changes. Those changes constitute the flow of meaning, which is so characteristic for semiosis in

[5]Peirce (1873).

general, although we do not fully grasp the meaning of it all. Modern semiotics is challenged to unfold this secret.

That challenge concerns another understanding of the *sign pool*: the most appropriate description and understanding of what texts and discourses are. Semiotics concerns the fact that "Two-way directions become multiple, various crossings among meanings are made possible, a patterning of meanings instead of one-to-one relationships appear realistic. Interdependency needs to provide a more precise knowledge of WHAT is interdependent with WHAT: 'particle' and 'total' are only two answers to those manifold 'what's' in question. Insightful knowledge of components seems therefore necessary. … The concept of a 'text' and of an interdependent 'word-meaning' complex are differently defined but treated as equal. It means that the semiotics of a text and the semiotics of meaning-holistic entities are considered equal and treated in parallel. … This reaches further than explaining meaning and meaning-holism by referring exclusively to words in a word-language. Meaning is more that words can say or can connect with."[6]

These remarks concern the theoretical dimensions of the new insights and fascination of the semiotics, which Kevelson initiated. A renewed focus on the *sign* might deepen our understanding and clarify the depth and width of that challenge. Greimas supported an understanding of the fact that signs are almost exclusively perceived and experienced when they are phenomena of the surface structure of the level of manifestation of texts and discourses. We seldom consider that this is not all! Signs are everywhere and it is difficult to acquire a reliable grip on texts and discourses as a totality in this approach. Signs are everywhere and, as Peirce noticed: everything. That does *not* concern solely signs at the surface, but also signs in signs below the surface of what we say or write. And in deep structures, signs are seldom already signs, but rather elements which are packed in broader sub-surface regions such as norms, values, expectations, social motives and the like, struggling to reach representation. Signs are born below surface, and only a social mechanism of selection allows them to be operational at the surface. Our interactive communication is therefore mostly about *what signs are going to be*, rather than about signs as fixed entities. Hence Peirce's dally to find the appropriate denomination of signs and the more than seventy proposals he left us as his heritage. This is the dynamics of semiotics: *the becoming is more important than the being*—and that is the crux of signs on every step at the path from sign to signification.

Is this important for legal semiotics? It is, and that forms a great challenge. The perhaps most important field of analysis and forthcoming research in legal semiotics concerns the traditional legal hermeneutics. Do not forget, that the hermeneutic approach is omnipresent in law, in philosophy, theory and practices of law, and it has a longstanding tradition with a well-determined pattern of searching the consequences of particular meanings laid down in words and speech. Texts and discourses are not static patterns or fixed fields of regulated verbal as well as

---

[6]On "sign pool": Broekman (2016), (OpCit), pp. 9, 208.

non-verbal behavior. This is what they often seem to be in traditional views and uses of law and legal practice.

A law text invites, so to say, to find one's way in authoritarian patterns of behavior. Hence Kevelson's repeated remarks in which she expresses her appreciation of a non-authoritarian attitude, which is forwarded in the semiotic approach to law. Other features of great importance evidently color texts and discourses because both are like plazas of a culture, fields in which subjects encounter. The "I say-v-You say" pattern is not experienced as a clash between opinions and powers but as an invitation to commonness in consideration and thought formation. The search for the originator of a law text, which should one literally follow in interpretation and application (in U.S. jurisprudence called 'originalism') is an example. In that view is the originator the dictatorial master of meaning rather than the host of consultation on situation-bound meanings. The contrast is clear, and the direction semiotics would favor is also clear. A fixed and obligated rule following of meaning is only possible with regard to surface concepts—signs included. But if one considers the wealth of spaces in which signs are in signs and related components which will- or will not appear to the surface of text and discourse, then one embraces an experience and attitude in which semiotics is a matter of *freedom* rather than of strict *rule following*. That freedom, in essence the freedom to create commonness, is the fascinating challenge if one unfolds the semiotic approach specifically in law and legal discourse. It forms the foundation for this Brief's plea to initiate further research into the Kevelson heritage.

References

Broekman JM and Backer LC (2015) Layered discourses, dynamic semiotics. In: Broekman JM & Backer CL (eds) Signs in law—a source book, Springer, Heidelberg, New York, Dordrecht, London

Broekman JM (2016) Meaning, narrativity, and the real. Springer, Switzerland

Broekman JM (2017) Verbal and non-verbal in semiotics. In: Semiotica. Journal of the International Association for Semiotic Studies (Issue 216), De Gruyter Mouton, p 19–40

Greimas AJ and Rastier F (1968) The interaction of semiotic constraints. In: Yale French Studies, Yale University Press

Kevelson R (1988) The law as a system of signs. Plenum Press, London/New York

Peirce CS (1873) On the nature of signs. www.commens.org/dictionary/term/sign

Part II
How

Chapter 3
Words, Signs and Signifying Concepts

Abstract The sign-character of legal expressions, unveiled by semiotic approaches, relates to the main features of the world around individuals and thus constitutes their biography. Major headlines of Kevelson's biography are presented in this chapter—her early empowering of women's emancipationist movements as well as her late academic and international scientific career. The latter lead to bibliographical notes and her perhaps not final bibliography we offer. However, this Brief provides a most recent, corrected and completed *Kevelson bibliography*, which is prepared in this chapter. Of importance is our observation that any such bibliography should consist in *two* parts: a *pre-academic* and an *academic* part. The first is lost and only vaguely mirrored in the second. Available data and techniques, as well as limitations of the work are thoroughly discussed. The most important signifying concepts are presented and discussed in this chapter; they are (a) dynamism, (b) textuality, and (c) pragmatism.

Keywords Bio/bibliography · Features of semiotics · Dynamics · Textuality Pragmatism

3.1 Words and Signs

In law, words are signs—and vice versa. Are they? Indeed: words function in law as the most predominant signs we can think of. Legal constituencies are created as signs of those signs, which importantly signify the fluid relations between objects, occurrences and interpretive communities. Legal semiotics may unveil what really happens. Lawyers search for signs, which can often be found in spoken or written words and texts. Every expression belonging to that field of interpretation changes object and sign at stake. This fluidity of law and legal discourse confirms the fluidity of legal texts despite the fact that texts do confirm in general a fixation as their main attitude. The flow that fascinates lawyers can be indicated: it is the flow from sign to signification. Judges, lawyers, lawmakers and politicians recognize the importance of the various styles and experiences that touch and change signs until

J.M. Broekman and F. Fleerackers, *Legal Signs Fascinate*, SpringerBriefs in Law,
https://doi.org/10.1007/978-3-319-69520-4_3

they are shining significations. Words are signs in law, and the words as signs flow constantly under the surface of signs as words: as 'I', 'me', 'we' as well as 'obligation', 'right', 'property' or 'cause', 'consequence' or even 'man' and 'human', realty' or 'matter'. Who will ever study those words as signs in law and in laws' many *vice versa's*—and how?

Yet, do not forget that humans have been fascinated by the wealth of relations between their own lives and those of the objects with their signs around them. Are these two fields mirroring? Such fascinations appear to be older than the words once gathered in grammars or syntaxes. They are perhaps older in the form of symbols created by the human hand. Their desire to control those words and with that control also the discourse of institutions like law is, in archeological terms, rather young. Living a life that accepts symbolic levels of articulation requires signs before it involves in words. The fascination we prompt is the fascination of a youth: difficult to control, powerful in its unruliness, rich in its unrealistic desires. 'How to share this' forms a challenge for each legal practitioner. The challenge also influenced the Critical Legal Studies movement in the last decade of the 20th century.[1]

In this light, the consideration seems reasonable, why one will ever focus on semiotics in law, and not on legal liability, personhood, justice, legal correctness or logic in the first place? Those issues would be socially and scientifically more relevant, it seems. Everyone entering the law's discourse might encounter them, whereas nobody will be urged to begin considerations on meaning in a semiotic context. Yet, one has to keep in mind that legal practitioners have no other instruments to unfold in their profession than *language*, broader formulated: than *linguistic articulations*. They not only perform their task within the limits of that social burden but they are also determined by the limits of their professional—as well as natural language. It is throughout possible that they change the character of naturalness of their words, for instance by means of professionalizing their expressions, but they have to keep reference to the natural language that happens to be the context of their activity. It means in essence, that they are bound by *meanings articulated by means of linguistic concepts*.

Lawyers can give names to occurrences, even without our (laymen, citizens) understanding—but those names are founded in a "say for law" of a judge, with emphasis on the *saying*. In other words: there exists no unsayable law, nor any mystic source for application of laws or for legislation. The conclusion fascinates: law is *exclusively* tied to linguistic articulation. Is that a stable bridge towards the study of a theory of sign and meaning, called semiotics?

This is one of the themes that inspired Roberta Kevelson on the basis of the philosophy of Charles S. Peirce and the possibility of exploring a discipline she called "semiotics of law" which focuses on "legal semiotics", more or less at distance from literary semiotics or from other forms of signs linked to a particular discipline. Kevelson is internationally and interdisciplinary acknowledged as the founder of semiotics of law being a special branch of the humanities. She

[1]On her appreciation of the Critical Legal Theory movement: Kevelson (1990), p. 133ff.

introduced the term during her post-doctoral tenure at Yale University and promoted international and cross-disciplinary studies of the field in English language since 1984. After her death in 1998, she left an impressive amount of papers, notes, photocopies and project designs in her office at Penn State University.[2] That treasure was brought to Texas Tech University but it remained unattended for more than a decade. Exactly those materials can form the basis for a renewed study of the theme and a refreshed fascination for signs and their basis in the context of modern humanities.

One should, however, not be shortsighted and understand Kevelson's proposal and plea for semiotics of law as an act without any historical and cultural embedding. Her observations and research must be find its place in a future, more encompassing cultural study, and must begin with the Significs Movement of Victoria Lady Welby's publications on Meaning as well as Significance, and in particular the influential role of her 1911 *Encyclopedia Britannica* article on Significs.[3] Implications of a *legal* semiotics were more or less in parallel to this article unfolded in the work of Jacob Israel de Haan, a lawyer and outstanding member of the Dutch *Signifische Beweging*.[4] A comparative study on the works of De Haan and Kevelson is still an unfulfilled wish.[5] Such an in-depth research would illustrate that her understanding of semiotics in general and their application in legal theory was founded on a broader interpretation of semiotics as a specific technical discipline. That view is shared with and several decades earlier outlined by De Haan. But the insights in the broader and more foundational topics appear to be very different. The latter were in the case of Kevelson clearly in parallel with the philosophy of Peirce, whereas De Haan's more encompassing philosophical views focused on epistemological issues and Neo-Kantian philosophy in general. It must be noticed in this context, that Kevelson's (1988) slogan pertaining to "law as a system of signs" was widely misunderstood. She does certainly *not* identify law with a system as understood in economy, technical sciences or systems theory, and signs were for her *not* fixed entities with which systems could become operative in society. Especially the background formed by a philosophy of language is important here. She formulates clearly that her introduction to "the law as a system of signs merely scratches the surface of a new universe of discourse." What she calls *the* law is apparently a specific discourse—and that insight requires a specific view on and understanding of language. She refers back to European philosophy,

[2]Chapter 6, Appendix A.

[3]Welby (1911), p. 78ff. and in Broekman and Backer (2015), (Op. Cit.), p. 43ff.

[4]Broekman and Backer (2015), (Op. Cit.), p. 27ff. On De Haan: Id. 51–89.

[5]Kevelson may have introduced the word "legal semiotics" but De Haan has certainly been more than half a century earlier in making the concept operative in legal theory and legal practice, especially in 1916, the year of his Doctoral Dissertation on the subject and his Inaugural Lecture in the discipline under the heading of "legal significs". Kevelson knew about his work from hearsay and did support a future English translation, as one of her office notes indicates. The English translation was, however, deferred and in 2015 made and published by Broekman in Signs of Law, (Op. Cit.), Part II, 27–89.

especially existentialism, before World War II while saying: "Clearly, with respect to this universe of discourse we are at such a primitive stage as our forebears were when they discovered existence". This localization challenges a more general view on philosophy of culture, in which specific methodologies were embraced in view of specific problem: "In approaching our task one attempts not to find the smallest indivisible element or subatomic particle of this phenomenon called a legal system, but rather to conceive first of all of the greatest and most general relationship. This approach resembles that of the functional linguists, for example, as contrasted with the linguistic method of transformational or generative grammar. This approach is also in marked contrast to that of the positivists, who begin with the single most general concept and then proceed to break it down into its constituent parts. Semiotics is both analytic and synthetic…".[6]

The latter words are spoken and written in great difference with De Haan; they bear autobiographical importance, since her life was in two different phases of fate and development rich in experiences of *dialogue*. Dialogues were axial to her and her life situation: first, as a powerful initiator of feminist features in the US East Coast region, and later in her academic career at Penn State University. Semiotics blossomed because of her acknowledging the inter-human and interactive value of dialogue. Speech acts that were performed in clusters of significance created newly articulated and unheard speech activities, meanings and opinions.

Hence the emphasis on the dynamic character of semiotics: the latter should be understood as the act of walking the path from sign to significance. Any research in that field is not characterized by a method that studies fixed and frozen entities, causalities between them, speech phenomena pertaining to them, but in contrast to this image is semiotics a performance itself: the performance of a challenge that envisages changes, moves, varieties, for short: otherness.

3.2 Biographical Notes on Roberta Kevelson

It seems quite exceptional that a concept called 'legal semiotics' and its position in the humanities—in particular a position between two ancient and well-respected disciples: philosophy and law—are engendered by one person and within the short time of one-and-a-half decade. That is in itself already an argument to establish a precise and well-documented biography. Until now, this has never been undertaken, neither in the Anglo-Saxon world nor elsewhere.[7] The papers mentioned in the above lines are most certainly of importance within the framework of such an attempt.

---

[6]Kevelson (1988), p. 298.

[7]A major attempt and until now the only one is: Pencak and Palecek (2002) in particular p. 141ff.: A Conversation with Roberta Kevelson. Also: Pencak and Lindgren (1998), p. 329f.

Roberta Kevelson was born November 1931 in Fall River, Massachusetts, married at the age of 17, raised four kids and had been selling real estate, wrote fiction, poetry and pieces of theater, participated in theater groups such as the Trinity Players of Providence, Rhode Island, and was active in the women's movement in her place of birth. She founded the women's center in Fall River and from there supported many extensions of the women's movement in Massachusetts. As President of the Community College in that same town, she took care of finding places and buildings for the college, as well as resources, budgets and communication channels such as columns in local journals, programs on TV and radio, and federal grants.

Since a word like 'emancipation' or 'movement' was unknown and its ideas unwelcome in that period, her grass-roots conferences were unique. One should study all the in's and out's of that culturally interesting period of time, and how she transformed her participation in that cultural period into a most interesting socio-political and historical case, which is worth studying in our days of emancipation and activism, not in the least because her forms of activism are of importance for today's studies of activist movements.

A future author writing a complete biography should explain how her energy and attention was first focusing on those issues and only later transformed in a successful manner when she co-founded, sponsored and served the International Association for the Semiotics of Law as well as the International Journal for the Semiotics of Law. But her Fall River activities were the beginnings, and law and legal discourse were not yet present, as we would expect from our perspective shaped by her publications and functions of the last decades of the century. In the framework of her women's center activities "she had helped revitalize older women (and men) who no longer felt themselves a part of society by getting them to interpret headlines and write letters to the editors of newspapers" Pencak noted.[8] But that was only one aspect of her emancipation- and feminist activities.

Her town of birth, Falls River, Massachusetts, was in need of a museum, which she established. In that town were—Pencak remembers—at least five different Portuguese communities, which received her support and attention, and the museum was one of the many means to reach that goal. In the mid-seventies she decides "to go back to school": first to Brown University graduate school to study linguistics, then to Cambridge, Massachusetts to enter the Orson Wells Film School. She could do so because in earlier years she already obtained a bachelor's degree from Goddard College, were she had experienced the Goddard College Community Radio, a community-based, non-commercial, listener-supported educational radio station with nearly 70 volunteer programmers who live and work in central and northern Vermont. In 1978 she received her doctorate degree, the first that embraces basic notions of semiotics. From there, her intellectual- and emotional life was directed towards academic tasks and the many social experiences that surround academics.

---

[8]Pencak (2002), (Op. Cit.), p. 142.

At this point an interim remark might inspire a future biographer. The constellations in Kevelson's life are interesting. Her name "Bobby" was already widely known in her feminist and emancipation period and that remained *in academia*. And that directs our attention to the socio-political circumstances of her life and academic career. She, not unlike a substantial number of US women, was during the last decade of the 20th century fascinated by the main ideas of the Critical Legal Studies Movement. But her life developed in an opposite direction: were the majority of woman, particularly woman-lawyers, going their path of life from legal studies and above all from legal education to feminism as a substantial theme and even the spirit of law, Bobby walked her path of life in another direction: from the feminist battleground into another, rather unknown semiotic criticism pertaining to law.

This difference in direction has to be researched within the framework of a future Kevelson biography. In contrast to contributors to the Critical Legal Studies movements, she presented legal discourse as an exemplary semiotic discourse. That presentation colored her attitude, her travels, her congress participation (especially the international congresses of the IVR.[9]) as well as her publications. It implies, that while studying semiotic, she changed emphasis on knowledge, consciousness and culture into emphasis on forms of articulation (literature in the first place), furthermore on social order, emancipation and politics. Bobby expanded that change of direction during her lifetime in a global perspective that included *women in semiotics*. One remembers in the first place the Victoria Lady Welby in London, who inspired not only Ch. S. Peirce and hence Bobby, but also in the US Susanne K. Langer, Margaret Mead and Ethel M. Albert. Those names parallel the Critical Legal Studies feminism and share the movement's ideas and ideals.

So far the interim remark. In the period preceding her doctorate, Bobby had written and published two books: her first was entitled *Style, Symbolic Language Structure, Syntactic Change*, published in the Peter de Ridder Press and its Publications in Semiotics of Language Vol. 2, Lisse, The Netherlands 1976. This publication mirrors her fascination by *changes* in language that occur in sciences as well as in daily life, its causes and forms of communication, such as questions and answers in conversation. No wonder that these themes had brought her from life experiences and hopes that were essential to feminism of those days to linguistic and meaning analyses. The book already marks intuitions and evolutions, which were coming true in later years. Her second book, published in 1977 also by Peter De Ridder Press in cooperation with the "Research Center for Language and Semiotic Studies" of Indiana University, was entitled: *Inlaws/Outlaws. A Semiotics of Systemic Interaction: "Robin Hood" and the "King's Law"*. Unnecessary to remark, that also this study reflected her extended experiences in conversations with a great diversity of people that marked her years of emancipation activities. The concept of 'law' introduced in this context is not in conformity with the ideas of

[9]IVR = Internationale Vereinigung für Rechts– und Sozialphilosophie; International Association for the Philosophy of Law and Social Philosophy.

law, which a lawyer exploits in his daily practice. Kevelson fortified the concept of legal semiotics in this text in her demonstration of the ways in which the outlawed Robin Hood ballads reinforced English Common Law.

So, the year at Yale as a post-doctoral fellow had begun with already two publications, which displayed an extraordinary level of thought and a rather new philosophical approach. Another post-doctoral year back at Brown University followed before her appointment at Penn State University in 1981. She founded the Penn State Center for Semiotic Research and began to organize her Round Tables in 1987, which included many scholars from Europe and other regions of the globe.[10] The Proceedings of the Round Tables were published annually; they were made public together with further important book publications on themes of Peirce's philosophy, on the dimensions of his pragmatism and on issues of legal semiotics embedded in themes of wider cultural importance. The latter: Proceedings of the Round Tables and publications of her own hand, were supported by at least two types of fascination she cherished during her many travels in the US, in Europe, the Near East, Latin America and other places: *participating* in congresses and thus finding out what colleagues and others think and do via conversations all over the world, and *lecturing* at Penn State and other institutions, so that students could become privileged partners in her conversation. Those two profiled her academic years at Penn State: her Center and the many National and International Conferences, where her presence and conversations were highly appreciated.[11]

When she spoke, or was writing, the philosopher Charles S. Peirce was with her. He was present in her thoughts, not as a Master nor as a Slave but as a most precious equal in relation to her understanding of life, its signs and many significations. So it is not surprising that the short period after she became Emeritus Professor at Penn State University in 1996, while continuing her Visiting Scholarship at the Philosophy Department of the College of William and Mary in Williamsburg, Virginia, more than one publication was an attempt to deepening her understanding of Peircean philosophy—his pragmatism not in the least. Month before she died in 1998, she completed her book *Peirce and the Mark of the Gryphon* that was published in 1999 with an introduction of her life-long comrade and former assistant, the historian William Pencak. Claw prints of the gryphon, Pencak suggests, are *the mark of the mark*—they are triangular *and* semiotic. That mark characterizes Roberta Kevelson's life: her final book tells a short story that she has written over thirty years before. Fascinations remain life long. They continue.

---

[10]An elaborate insight into the features and organization of Kevelson's "Round Tables" is in Broekman and Mootz (2011), p. 9ff. and in: Brigham (1999), p. 333ff.

[11]Jurists who read about Kevelson's Round Tables consider their presence as a treasure; but they were not manifold, and the influence of the Round Tables in the world of legal practitioners was limited. For that reason is this Brief In Law a message remembering them that recent memories and experiences of friends and colleagues can become a most valuable component of one's professional- and private life.

3.3 Bibliographical Notes on Roberta Kevelson

It seems important to publish a bibliography of Roberta Kevelson's publications in the context of this study. *There exists until now no definitive bibliography*, and this attempt to provide such a document should also be read with some restrictive remarks in mind. The first is, that one should be aware of the fact that a bibliography of Kevelson's work concerns hitherto solely her *academic* texts. A bibliography of *all* published texts appears impossible. Such a bibliography would include all texts, journal contributions, flyers, notes and other materials she produced before unfolding her academic career. The texts related mainly to her activities connected with female emancipation and women movements are difficult to obtain. The question is whether there would be any interest in those papers and whether any social relevance would be powerful enough to support such a project. *Any bibliography of Kevelson should consist in two parts:* the *pre-academic* texts functioning in her wide-ranging social activism, and the *academic texts* functioning in her professorial career, mainly at Penn State University from 1981 on and at the College of William and Mary, Williamsburg, Virginia, from 1991 on.

We described in the preceding paragraph Roberta Kevelson's powerful activism as linked to multiple and multifarious texts. It was mentioned how she wrote fiction, poetry and pieces of theater, participated in theater groups such as the Trinity Players of Providence, Rhode Island, and was active in the women's movement in her place of birth. She founded the women's center in Fall River and from there supported many extensions of the women's movement in Massachusetts. As President of the Community College in that same town, she wrote columns in local journals, programs on TV and radio, and pleas for obtaining federal grants. Those textual activities, in themselves a clear sign for her unfolding social activism, would belong to her bibliography. But they are never collected, published together and analyzed as precious components of the US mid-20th century activism. On the contrary: even William Pencak, her assistant and close friend, mentioned these papers without ever publishing or discussing them.[12] They are lost. One has to accept this conclusion despite the fact that their study would, have been an important contribution to the study of social activism in the North Eastern United States during the forties and fifties of the preceding century. And what is more: theoretical notions of sign, significance and semiotics in the field of activism would have been studied in the light of her views—it would have illustrated that social activism needs also in our days continuously renewed basic theory design.[13]

We thus have to conclude that a bibliography in the case of Kevelson is solely an *academic* bibliography. It is founded on (1) the bibliographical data and techniques available, which are (2) closely connected with biographical issues (the academic career), and (3) the fact that this bibliography is limited to specific academic works (which also illustrates the lack of high-level analyses and data-provisions) despite

[12]Pencak and Lindgren (1998), p. 329.

[13]Annelies and Broekman (2017), pp. 112–134.

the fact that one encounters in this bibliography some of the most important origins of the legal semiotics discipline.

3.3.1 Bibliographical Data and Techniques

There are *four* different remarks to be made regarding the quality of bibliographical data pertaining to Kevelson's academic texts.

(a) It is remarkable that her bibliographical data are (also in her proper publications) represented by sometimes very different mentions in footnotes, references and book-bibliographies. Years of publication often differ in connection with often only fragmentarily published titles of books or essays. Page numbers are sometimes incorrect or erroneously mentioned—not only in her own books but also in essays on her work from her closest cooperator William A. Pencak.
(b) The office papers, mentioned in the above text, do at this moment not provide enough support to compensate these flaws. They are not yet systematically ordered and it seems that Kevelson as author has not paid much attention to the bibliographical implications of her writings.
(c) We have to add to the description of this problematic situation, that there are no reports available nor texts or drafts of lectures and other presentations Kevelson offered to the many Congresses she visited, among which for instance the worldwide meetings of the IVR—which were regularly published in the "Archives for Philosophy of Law and Social Philosophy"—or the various Semiotic societies.
(d) A special topic of bibliographical importance is the almost yearly organization of Round Tables in the framework of her Penn State University's Center for Semiotic Research. With colleagues throughout the world, she organized discussions and data exchanges since 1987, and a guess is, that in the years until 1995 more than 150 scientists participated. Each volume of those Round Table publications has their Index, but *an Index of those Indexes* is never made, nor is there any encompassing study of that material. The many contributions covered the final decades of the 20th century—a period with many "post—" movements like post-structuralism, post-modernism, post-feminism, which all exhibited their specific views on the next millennium—views that are in fact lost in the seldom complete availability of the Round Table publications and the lack of an full-scale overview.

3.3.2 Biography and Bibliography

There are noticeable gaps between biographical situations and biographically noticed outcomes.

(a) The globally known and appreciated Round Tables on Semiotics of Law are important in that regard, but not an exception in clearly showing this gap. As always in the life situations of writers and scientists, there are close ties between the actual period of life and the publications. That is most profiled in *editorial work*, as the many contributions of Roberta Kevelson clearly illustrate. No overview of the editorial work as a member of the Board of the *Journal of Philosophy and Rhetoric* and the *International Journal for the Semiotics of Law* exists, although this would have been providing an interesting component of her bibliography. The same is true for her activity as Editor-in-Chief of the eleven volumes of the Peter Lang publications entitled *Critic of Institutions*—some of those volumes are included in the bibliography that is presented here, but there is also no orientation concerning specific Kevelson texts and related activities. While consulting the bibliography in this publication, one should also be aware of the lack of information regarding to the eight volumes of the Peter Lang Series *Law and the Human Sciences.*

(b) The bibliography delivers facts created in her *academic* life period, but those texts are by no means the only ones she conceived. However, texts written *before* she begun her academic career seem to be lost, are unknown and only fragments may be contained in the boxes with office papers as mentioned before. They can never appear in the final bibliography, despite the fact that they have played an important role in the life of this distinguished author.

William Pencak visited her in November 1996, the year of her emeritus status, when she still was a Visiting Scholar at the College Of William and Mary in residence. She told him how she had mentioned to the Dean of the Community College in Fall River, who interviewed her because of her application for the function of director of the women's center, that until then she "talked and wrote"—among many other issues interesting her, on history, music, philosophy and semiotics.[14] Words performed their task of Consciousness Raising; words spoken as well as words written had this social effect, she experienced. That particular experience, unfolded in at least two decades *before* she begun to explore her academic career that formed the basis for this bibliography, formed the truth that bridged the two periods before- and after her 1981 nomination as a Professor and Director of the Center for Semiotic Research at the Pennsylvania State University. Let us keep in mind that this experience will forever remain beyond the picture presented by this bibliography.

3.3.3 Limitations

Finally, there is a clear sign to be understood in the context of this entire bibliography. It is the fact, that a bibliography can only contain specifically published

[14]Pencak and Lindgren (1998), (Op. Cit.), p. 329f.

texts. It was made clear, that this document does not embrace all sorts of engagement that unfolded beyond the publishing procedure. As a consequence, we must underline that there are for instance no texts available—neither for publication in the bibliography nor for the reader to consult—that are directly linked with Kevelson's *visiting appointments*, such as appointments at the Princeton University, Cambridge University, University of Virginia Law School, University of Edinburgh, University of New Mexico, or her experiences as Vice-President and President of the Semiotic Society of America. Words must have been spoken, notes written, remarks included in papers, advices formulated. They are altogether experienced by the author and by her hearer without traces that can be incorporated in a bibliography. Yet they belong to that document—biographic, as a sign of memory beyond print.

Those three limitations should be considered if one consults the revised, corrected, completed and edited bibliography in Chap. 7, Appendix B in this Brief.

3.4 Signifying Concepts

After considerations of biographical occurrences and a bibliographical overview, we need to provide additional insight into some of the basic concepts Roberta Kevelson explored in her philosophical and semiotic work pertaining to law and legal discourse. A most direct and literal access to those concepts was made available in William Pencak's "From **A**bsurdity to **Z**en", a publication in which a large list of words indicates what concepts were important by means of literal quotations from her texts. On the other hand, a Legal Semiotics Vocabulary is available since the 2013 publication of the Second Volume in the Springer Series "The Semiotics of Law in Legal Education". The latter does not include legal terms, but solely semiotic expresses involved in major legal uses, and refers to at least *five* other dictionaries.[15]

The title of this chapter should lead us towards a short presentation of her work profile: *concepts signify*. What does that mean? There are at least three extremely important concepts in Kevelson's oeuvre that can bring us towards a unique understanding of semiotics and its place in modern philosophy—the result of the task she had given herself to perform in ways that was never achieved before—and just reaching beyond the limits of law and legal discourse. They pertain to (1) the concept of *dynamism*, (2) the concept of *textualism*, and (3) the concept of *pragmatism*.

[15]Pencak and Palecek (2002), (Op. Cit.), pp. 49–139, Broekman and Backer (2013) (Op. Cit.), p. 233f.

3.4.1 Dynamism

The challenge to reach beyond the limits of law in order to acquire knowledge of law is not naïve and guides us towards the realm of conceptualizations; a realm that is deeply characterized by the *dynamics* of semiotic thought formation. Signs are not fixed things—in that regard is it incorrect to talk about traffic–'signs' because traffic is fluent, signs are fluent and the function of signs in traffic is to keep that traffic fluent! Peirce did certainly not consider a sign as a means to fixate reality when he claimed that "everything can become a sign". On the contrary, the expression involves us in the fact that reality will never be fixed, neither by words nor by signs. If that fixation could occur, then the path from sign to signification would be blocked before one could walk it. For this reason, she often repeats and even more often underlines that the semiotic process is *evolutionary* by definition. Here is the cause for the fact that a sign alone cannot exist, just like a human being alone cannot be understood as truly human. Signs need to be Contextual, to be inherently Otherness, to be on its way to become Different.

If concepts characterize and help sciences or philosophical insights unfold, then they embrace sign–properties. In doing so, evolution in sciences as well as in philosophy is not an additional color but an inherent feature of both. Semiotics will confirm this, profit from this insight and prove the importance of the multiple discourses humans experience and sciences explore. A deep insight seems hidden in this conclusion. It is an insight that is concentrated in the concept of synthesis, as the semiotics of Kevelson always underlined. The fact is, that signification and meaning, valuation and information do not evolve through authoritarian behavioral or autocratic summation of articulations. They *evolve*, and evolve mainly through verbal and lingual interaction, above all through the never-ending shifts of authority from speaker to hearer, who themselves are components of a community, which is in its turn a fragment of culture.

An example can be found in the heart of semiotic explorations.

Remember the famous French/Lithuanian semiotician A.J. Greimas, already mentioned in Part I, who is not solely known for his "semiotic squares" but also for his attempt to understand how structures of a discourse organize themselves into a narrative.[16] This, one could say, is essential for lawyers who care about being confronted with texts of the law and society's need to have them interpreted. Chomsky had already differentiated in the context of his idea of a generative grammar between the *surface structure* and the *deep structure* of a sentence, but never mentioned a text or a narration. His reference to a possible differentiation between surface and deep structures keeps the inherent reference to a fixed and dualistic speaker–hearer situation intact, and that is, as Greimas and later Kevelson underlined, in semiotic perspective absolutely untenable.

To emphasize this viewpoint, Greimas used "the journey" as principal metaphor for an unfolding human life: "… we can imagine that the human mind, in order to

[16]Broekman and Backer (2015), (Op. Cit.), pp. 9, 129.

achieve the construction of a cultural object (literary, mythical, pictorial, etc.) starts with simple elements and follows a complex course (…) Our aim is to give a rough idea of that course. It may be considered to move from immanence to manifestation in three principal stages: *deep structures*, which define the fundamental mode of an individual or a society (…), *superficial structures* constitute a semiotic grammar system (…) and *structures of manifestation*, which produce and organize the significances."[17] This picture has become shorthanded in semiotic literature to a differentiation between *surface*- and *deep* structure of a text, or (as Julia Kristeva highlighted.[18]) between *phenotext* and *genotext*. But is just *saying* that this is a journey and not a positioning of fixated concepts enough to understand not only the determinations called "surface and depth structure" but also (and perhaps above all) the fluid moves from surface to depth and vice versa?

There is indeed an important consideration in this semiotic insight. The distinctions mentioned by Greimas and Kristeva, each of them somewhat inspired by Chomsky, should not lead to the belief that they pertain to two enriching, separated, fixated and rather independent concepts in linguistics and the meaning making process in a culture. On the contrary: the two are solely indications of what Kevelson qualified as "the dynamics" of semiotics. Hence the remark of Kristeva, that a text is not a linguistic phenomenon but the *engenderment* of such a phenomenon. That leads to a different insight into the qualities of a text, which is of course extremely important for *legal* texts. Take for instance the US Supreme Court oral argument. It *precedes* a written and printed, definitive and surface judgment. In the "oral argument" is the process of engenderment of a text on its way to become an institutionally accepted surface. The oral arguments seem often less important than the written briefs: spoken words seem in the minds of judges and lawyers in Court to have less weight than written.

Kevelson would embrace a major conclusion drawn from this example. Meanings engender from *entanglements* of linguistic nature. Reading and understanding is a form of that entanglement. The latter are beacons of the journey, Greimas told us; they are the *dynamics* Kevelson highlighted, and they inspired her to repeat what Peirce once remarked: the engenderment of a meaning is not a fixated issue but a *film*. Kristeva deepened that metaphor, when she formulated how linguists and semioticians should also study the signifying processes in their *ethical* relevance.

3.4.2 *Textuality*

The step from there to the particular position of "the text" in Kevelson's legal semiotics project is not a surprise. Surface– and deep structures of a text are never

[17] Greimas and Rastier (1968), p. 86ff.

[18] Kristeva (1969), p. 278ff.

separate layers but constituting a text by means of their togetherness, through their special relations, which have been a riddle to the philosophers and scientists alike. Kevelson compares, again inspired by Peirce, the dynamics that keep the two structures together with the fascination of the alchemists and refers to Paracelcus. She wrote: "What Peirce refers to as the key to the riddle of human understanding, the old alchemists spoke of as the '*mysterium coniunctionis*' (…) The mystery of the conjunction is at the heart of all alchemical experimentation: it is that of philosophy, of science, of each person in search of an alchemist, a play, a role, a place, an address. (…) All sign–interpretation consists of a synthesis that melds these two universes, that conjoins them to produce a new, more complex whole."[19] In her critical questioning how it is possible that one can try to have grip on sections of a text without caring for the interdependence of those sections, and thus the text as a whole, she walks the difficult path towards a new understanding of what a text—in particular a text in law—in essence is.

That consideration is not solely philosophical: during the 2017 Confirmation Hearing of the US Senate Judiciary Committee, Judge Neil Gorsuch was asked about his attitude towards a Constitution text or a law text in general. The majority of listeners, mainly members of the Judiciary Committee, expected information about "*interpreting* a text of law"—but that answer did not come. Judge Gorsuch pointed out that a text, also text in law, is in the first place a privileged and specified *area of encounter*. Interpreting a text, Kevelson would have added to Judge Gorsuch's formulation, is encountering a large number of opinions, traditions, views, habits, beliefs, confusions and desirability's, which are altogether formatted in a mode of fixation (the opinion) to mask the character of "being woven". "We spin yarns in legal narratives and court cases," she had added.[20] And, this insight opens up to an even more radical view on texts: the latter are particular *spaces*—texts are *open spaces*. The fight about meaning is a fight about occupying a particular section in space. That is clear and effective, since "in legal dialogue the properties of the stage—bench, bar, inner space of the court etc. —define it in relation to commonplace living space and in fact oppose it to all trivialized, pleasure space. The law, or logical space, is set apart in precisely the same way that a clearing for religious rites or a house of worship is traditionally marked in relation to its contextual surrounding community space." A conclusion Kevelson offers, is clear: "The language of the law is a jargon improvised to sound strange."

Today, we would agree that the language of law is an artificial language, which is often and fragmentarily reformulated in a natural language—but by no means 'improvised'. Kevelson tried already four decades earlier, in 1977, to describe how "Semantic signs which related to Law were produced analogically and encoded into conventional law language. Implied is that the 'geno-textual' reference is the play structure characterized by conflict, conventional rules of strategy, and the element

[19]Kevelson (1996), pp. 13, 14, 129ff.

[20]Kevelson (1993), p. 56.

of chance. In other words, law language signifies the signified hermeneutic code of the sacred play."[21] Texts are not to obey in accordance with their literal content, but they are anchor places in space: always elsewhere, always on the move, always in the mode of encounter.

These intuitions became confirmed some three decades later in a special 2006 issue of the *International Journal for the Semiotics of Law*, dedicated to *The Spaces and Places of Law*. In Richard Mohr's philosophically fascinating contribution, the State is presented as "*the floating signifier*" and its idea/ideology of the separation of powers "signifies so much that its specific denotations could never exhaust the possibilities: there will always be some remainder, some possible meaning which is not enacted. (Which never *could* be enacted because it is a *mystery.*)" Indeed, "the question of law's effective constitution of the floating signifier of the state is both a pragmatic question for the political sociology of law, and a theoretical question for semiotics". Mohr proceeds: "If the floating signifier was 'the guiding concept of the human sciences in the twentieth century'—as Agamben suggested—it is time to explore the possibility of *exactly the opposite* relationship between the sign and its meaning, through a reading of the quotidian reinterpretation of the legal signifiers of state power."[22] That leads, according to Mohr, to the study of a spatial semiotics of law and the state. Predominant in that question is to observe how spatial signifiers promote the state as a legal fiction—a viewpoint that was in 1993 underlined in Kevelson study on Peirce.

A conclusion is clear: her understanding of a text as a linguistic entity, and a legal text as such an entity transferred into the artificial language of the law, is basic for her fundamental insight into the *dynamic* character of semiotics. She underlines how the text–phenomenon is surprisingly near to the concept of *human interrelation* as well as of *interactivity*. A *legal* text emphasizes what is characteristic for any text in any cultural context: a text is a *place, a space, a 'topos'* to coordinate human views, life styles, habits, traditions, knowledge, meaning, order, discipline or regulation. Being in that space is far more, and has a far wider significance than the word 'interpretation' of a text suggests. It emphasizes a particular dimension of semiotic nature, which is also widening what is generally considered as *legal hermeneutics*. Kevelson's semiotic insight in the essence of the legal text broadens that hermeneutic perspective. That view remains within the traditional support for the idea of a legal order in general and the State in particular. The judgment of a Judge cannot be private or arbitrary, but has to accept a legally acknowledged deliberation of all constitutive factors of a life situation as such. Any legal order accepts the order of its legal texts: this rule has to be interpreted as a *spatial* given.

The interesting issue in this broader understanding of the concept of the textual is not directly concerning the *text*, but rather the closely connected concept of the *speech act*. The parallel is obvious, and Kevelson explained this in a number of different cultural and literary contexts, among others as early as her 1977

[21]Kevelson (1977), p. 38f.

[22]Mohr (2006), p. 241, Agamben (2005), p. 37.

Inlaws/Outlaws publication. *Text* and *speech* are both characterized by the *spatial* features of their specific forms of interactivity. A *writer–reader* relation parallels a *speaker–hearer* relation; both have parallel and often the same name: John is writer and speaker in relations with Sarah, who as a reader and hearer gives the writing and speaking a sense, vice versa. The traditional dualistic view in social philosophy and philosophy of language has fixed positions, which should create the opposite: John and Sarah are in text and speech *signs* of the spatial complexity of the two. A speech act is never a deed that the hearer of that speech activity has to undergo passively: even the speech act that excels in one-sidedness, for instance of a dictator or an absolute ruler, takes care of and depends upon the presence of the *other*—although that *caring* and that *otherness* are perverted in this case. Text and speech, the speech act included, are solely possible thanks to the *interactivity* functioning in those two manifestations of inter-subjectivity. Semiotics provokes openness in communication especially in law, which in its turn puts the narrow-mindedness of the sender/receiver model in legal thought formation and its institutions in perspective.

This in-depth exploration of the concepts of text and speech in semiotic perspective makes Kevelson conclude, that there is even in the most totalitarian and repressive society *no* closed legal system. This is, because the position of the *other* in the speech act of a *self* cannot be left out, so that no person is ever a totally passive object of the law. The fundamental reason for this conclusion is more than once formulated in her widely spread and highly appreciated 1988 publication *The Law as a System of Signs*, in which one reads the argument: "… each person is not force-fed values and ideas but produces them in interaction with others. A person is a creator of signs and therefore of culture. (…) Legal 'commands' do not strike a person directly from the outside but are filtered through his subjective scale of straights and crooked." Being a component of text or speech, the act of a person is continuously "engaging in a communicative event, using signs in persuasive ways, toward some desired consequence". In this context, she reminds the reader an important Peircean opinion: "Every reinterpretation of a sign according to Peirce is really the creation of new meaning. Thus, the process of finding equivalences between legal signs from a cross-cultural perspective is the search for new meaning in the world".[23]

3.4.3 Pragmatism

There is a certain logic that leads to the concept of pragmatics and the specific philosophical approach called pragmatism. It has not to do with the fact that pragmatism became a trendy name at the end of the 20th century. But there are at least three remarks that make this path to pragmatism understandable:

[23]Kevelson (1988), p. 47.

(a) Kevelson's interest in the theme did not come into existence because of its fashionable position in philosophy and politics, but because of the many dimensions it opened in semiotic regions. In one of her three studies on Peircean pragmatism she remarks, how his method "is dramatistic, agonistic, engaging inner and outer in the problem of transforming/renewing/creating habits of truths, i.e., habits of value and meaning."[24] With these words, she explores the pragmatic dimension in the form of a study with focus on the uses and contexts of language.
(b) The recognition of the necessary position of the *other* in the very heart of the speech act is at the basis of this unfolding viewpoint. It initiates a power of renewal, which one can understand as a new form of pragmatism that should be understood as multi-dimensional and ultimately reach cosmic dimensions. "The business of pragmatism is to create the cosmos as a vast, living, growing, continually changing representation of intellectual energies: a light-and-sound show in which we, as our institutions–our complex and various modes of conduct–are the actors planning our happening, linking our lines, making our mazes ever more amazing (as Peirce describes) and spinning sense and sign into this adventure, this high adventure of *becoming*."[25] It is this *cosmic* experience that founded her interest in and emphasis on pragmatism.
(c) The latter comprises ultimately the totality of signifying, and is a final destination, a point that marks the path from sign to significance—the path to grasp as a shorthand definition of semiotics. The *epistemic* concern for meaning and sense appears in this light most prominent. But: it is also, and will remain forever, a path set up and experienced by *humans*. And *humans* are never *alone* —any philosophy that does not understand or simply leaves out this observation, is a failure. Here is, what Peircean thought formation brought Kevelson to understand.

One needs to concentrate on the most central issue at stake: *the unique combination of pragmatism's epistemic concern and the observation that no human being, no nothing is alone*! The latter is indeed clear in human consciousness but it includes all cosmic processes. Peirce notified the importance of his observation that every fragment of being needs an opposition to another in order to be itself. He writes: "… an object *exists*, if and only if, it reacts with every other existing object of the same universe" and "Existence is that mode of being which lies in opposition to another. To say that a table exists is to say that it is hard, heavy, opaque, resonant, that is, produces immediate effects upon the senses, and also that it produces purely physical effects, attacks the earth (that is, is heavy), dynamically reacts against other things (that is, has inertia), resists pressure (that is, is elastic), has a definite capacity for heat, etc." It thus follows, that "*A thing without oppositions* ipso facto *does not exist*."[26] That are Peirce's words for: nobody and nothing

[24]Kevelson (1998), p. 164f.

[25]Kevelson (1988), (Op. Cit.), p. 15.

[26]Hartshorne and Loess 1931–1958.

is *alone*; they inspired Kevelson not only in her writing and philosophical though formation, but also in the fulfillment of her educational tasks. Teaching, she remarked, should be "the creative exploration of ideas rather than the perfunctory presentation of accumulated wisdom, and students should be approached as adults by their teachers who invited them to sit down and learn with them".[27]

But there is more to say. *If nothing will be without it's opposite, nothing is without some other or without otherness in general.* Peirce and later also Kevelson relate that insight to the often envisaged distinction between Firstness, Secondness and Thirdness—a terminology that made Peircean thoughts accessible and popular because they suggested a cosmological relevance and the disclosure of problems about 'being'. The three are definitively modifications of a constitutive Otherness (even in the form of an 'opposite') without which reality is impossible although they display fundamentally different structures. That corresponds with Peirce's image of cosmos and reality: first there is chance, and the subject's being is positively regardless of anything else—which can only be a possibility, because any being is in this phase beyond any acting upon one another. Even the qualification itself is meaningless and what Peirce called "Firstness" is therefore "a flash", a not-yet-articulated process that may be or perhaps is not yet in processing. "In the idea of being, Firstness is predominant (…) on account of its self-containedness."[28] The latter word indicates, that an opposition does not play any role in Firstness, so that the latter is solely a fast over-blowing shadow, a flash, or a 'blitz' beyond power of constitution. Firstness fascinates and suggests explaining 'being' and 'all there is', but it clearly does not—because of its lack of opposition or otherness.

All this will never be experienced, viewed, registered or researched because it is a thought without ever reaching the level of reality, which Peirce called *Thirdness*. In Firstness, the *pragmata* volatilize before they become substantial because there is no *otherness*. Therefore, after Firstness, there is Secondness—if not: there is nothing, no substitutive Firstness nor anything else. Hence Peirce's 1887 remark: "The First is that whose being is simply in itself, not referring to anything nor lying behind anything. The Second is that which is what it is by force of something to which it is second."[29] Kevelson understood well: concrete things, *pragmata*, exist because they are always and in all possible forms entangled in a relation or a reaction upon others, and therefore characterized as *seconds*. Why is that called "seconds" and not "firsts", because "first" seems so concrete and important in comparison to the flashy and vacillating "second"? It is because of the cosmic relevance of the fact that there is always a relation between the thing itself (Kant) and its otherness, Peirce stated.

He thus underlined in the same *Guess at the Riddle*: "But we need not, and must not, banish the idea of the first from the second; on the contrary, the Second is precisely that which cannot be without the first. It meets us in such facts as Another,

[27]Pencak (2002), (Op. Cit.), p. 145.

[28]Peirce (1998c), p. 150ff., Broekman (2010), p. 37ff.

[29]Peirce (1998b) (1887/1888), (Op. Cit.), Vol. I, p. 248.

Relation, Compulsion, Effect, Dependence, Independence, Negation, Occurrence, Reality, Result. A thing cannot be other, negative, or independent, without a first to or of which it shall be other, negative, or independent."

In as far as *pragmatism* is concerned, we experience that all *pragmata* ('things' or 'data') belong to Secondness because they depend on the constitutive power of *otherness* in which Secondness is embedded. But our experience appears to be a form of representation, and therefore *sign* of *signs*—in Peircean terminology: *Thirdness*. The latter has in his thoughts a *mediating* function, which is truly concerning the cosmos in its totality: including human awareness and consciousness, all signs given and signs of signs through which we conceptualize realty and strive for a really *dynamic* pragmatism. "*Thirdness*, in the sense of the category, is the same as mediation", Peirce notes. "The *first* is agent, the *second* patient, the *third* is the action by which the former influences the latter. Between the beginning as first, and the end as last, comes the process which leads from first to last." That process is always a matter of reference, of constitution through the presence of Otherness.

The world of Thirdness as conceived on its own is therefore problematic, just because it excludes this referential function of otherness. The *Third Harvard Lecture on Pragmatism* tells us in this context: "The most degenerate Thirdness is where we conceive a mere Quality of Feeling, or Firstness, to represent itself to itself as Representation. Such, for example, would be Pure Self-Consciousness, which might be roughly described as a mere feeling that has a dark instinct of being a germ of thought. This sounds nonsensical, I grant."[30] Here it appears how central the issue of *reference to otherness* functions.

There are two aspects to finally mention, about Kevelson's studies on Peirce and Pragmatism. (1) The first is to understand the importance of *otherness*, which comes to the fore in any consideration of reality. There is no conscious consideration of 'a thing' without what Peirce's Secondness brought to the fore about this *constitutive event* called *oterness*. In the heart of 'meaning making' is that function of otherness. This constitutes the framework of *semiotics* since human life is a *sign-bound* event and its pragmatism concerns the steps from sign to signification to sign.

(2) The second aspect is even more complex: our thought formation is always a form of representation; thus concerns the sign of signs. We only experience, pragmatism tells us, *signs* of Firstness, Secondness and Thirdness. In that regard is semiotics (as the study of signs being an idea in a universe of ideas) always a matter of representation—or, more often: the hope and expectation to *master* that representation.

We conclude: those two observations together form the dynamics of Kevelson's attempts to unveil the relations in the triad, which are basic to any philosophy the name 'pragmatism' worthy. The latter emphasizes a progressing articulation of the foundational function of otherness in mediation—a truly cosmic issue to clarify. In

---

30 Peirce (1998a), (Op. Cit.), p. 161f.

how far exactly that mediation is the basis for conceiving reality must be the subject of a future study of Kevelson's semiotics in relation with pragmatism. That analysis will be a noteworthy expansion of our insight and knowledge of semiotics as a discipline in the human sciences and ultimately in a philosophical cosmology in which concepts unveil their power of signifying.

References

Agamben G (2005) State of exception, Chicago UP
Annelies E, Broekman JM (2017) The wealth of activism. In: DADA-Rivista Di Antropologia Post-Globale, Spec. Issue, Trieste, p 112–134
Brigham J (1999) Millennium reflexions: Roberta Kevelson and the law and semiotics round table. Int J Semiot Law 12(3)
Broekman JM, Backer LC (2015) Signs in law—a source book. Springer Dordrecht Heidelberg London New York
Broekman JM, Backer LC (2013) Lawyers making meaning. Springer, Dordrecht Heidelberg London New York
Broekman JM, Mootz III, Francis J (eds) (2011) The semiotics of law in legal education, Springer Dordrecht Heidelberg London New York
Broekman JM (2010) Firstness and phenomenology. In: Wagner A, Broekman JM (eds) Prospects of legal semiotics. Springer, Dordrecht Heidelberg London New York
Greimas AJ, Rastier Fr (1968) The interaction of semiotic constrains. Yale Fr Stud 41
Hartshorne C, Loess P (eds) (1931) The collected papers of Charles Sanders Peirce, vol 1. Principles of Philosophy, § 457, Harvard UP 1931–1958
Kevelson R (1977) Inlaws/Ooutlaws. A semiotics of systemic interaction. The Peter de Ridder Press, Lisse
Kevelson R (1990) Peirce, paradox, praxis., Mouton de Gruyter, Berlin/New York
Kevelson R (1996) Peirce, science, signs. Peter Lang Publisher, New York
Kevelson R (1993) Peirce's aesthetics of freedom. Peter Lang Publishers, New York/Bern
Kevelson R (1998) Peirce's pragmatism: the medium as method. Peter Lang Publisher, New York
Kevelson R (1988) The law as a system of signs. Plenum Press, New York/London
Kristeva J (1969) SEMEIOTIKÉ. Recherches pour une sémanalyse, Ed. du Seuil, Paris
Mohr R (2006) Living legal fictions: constituting the State or submerging the signifier?. Int J Semiot Law 19
Peirce CS (1998a) The categories defended. Harvard Lecture No 3, [April 9, 1903]. In: The essential Peirce, selected philosophical writings, vol 2. Indiana UP, Indianpolis & Bloomington
Peirce CS (1998b) A guess at the riddle. In: The essential Peirce, selected philosophical writings, vol 2. Indiana UP, Indianapolis and Bloomington
Peirce CS (1998c) On phenomenology, 2nd Harvard Lecture [April 2, 1903]. In: The Peirce edition project, Selected philosophical writings, vol 2. Indiana UP, Indianapolis and Bloomington
Pencak WA, Lindgren JR (1998) New approaches to semiotics and the human sciences, Appendix One, Peter Lang, New York etc.
Pencak W, Palecek C (2002) From Absurdity to Zen. The Wit and Wisdom of Roberta Kevelson, Peter Lang, New York
Pencak W (2002) A conversation with Roberta Kevelson. In: Pencak W, Palecek C (eds) From Absurdity to Zen. The Wit and Wisdom of Roberta Kevelson, Peter Lang, New York
Welby VL (1911) What is significs? The Encyclopedia Britannica 25

Chapter 4
Semiotics Education in Law

Abstract Considerations of 'education' fascinate in the case of Kevelson for various reasons. They do, however, also make limitations visible. Fascination and limitation go hand in hand, and form in this case a clear profile that initiates a plea to develop further research. This chapter focuses on the nature of Semiotics, furthermore on the implications of Kevelson's understanding of the concept of dialogue as a valuable contrast to other forms of communication, on a complete absence of any notion of the engenderment of Digital– or E–education and related forms of unfolding E–communication during the last decade of her scientific and educational activity, and the absence of personal educational experience in a Law School.

Keywords Otherness · Dialogue · E-education · Law school experience

4.1 The Nature of Semiotics

Kevelson's activities embraced a great variety of aspects, which were all related to language. She understood long before the unfolding of her academic career in how many regards language can be active in the world, shapes and mirrors history, and thus is also the basis for what we generally call 'education'. Otherness is always present in words (and above all in spoken words), she experienced during her support for the women's movement in Fall River, Massachusetts in the sixties and early seventies of the 20th century. An educational situation is unique because that otherness present in words or related linguistic utterances was in those years conceived by her long before electronic education became accepted and personalized. As a consequence, the presence of the other became exclusively concrete for her in the participant of the women movement, the student or the colleague in Congresses or during one of her many Round Tables. Seen from this angle, Kevelson's life was full of education opportunities—and thus reaching from early social movements to international and multilingual congress life.

J.M. Broekman and F. Fleerackers, *Legal Signs Fascinate*, SpringerBriefs in Law,
https://doi.org/10.1007/978-3-319-69520-4_4

Those opportunities and experiences were not without theoretical and, above all, not without philosophical interest. One should remember, how a very first attempt to deliver a biography of Kevelson, already highlighted her 1976 publications in which "organized chaos" was understood as a symbol of the realization of linguistic change.[1] One reads in the essay of William Pencak a text that brings a remarkable feature to the fore: it suggests that while we speak, we are obliged in our reasoning to cultivate a disposition that is hospitable toward contradictions, oppositions, cross-references and the like. This remark referred to Peirce's *Exact Logic*, which tells us that *facts can only exist in relation*, and that relation is most generally a contrast or contradiction to that which is not. Pencak warns us, that "unless her reader can develop not just a mere recognition of the logic of paradox, but an empathetic understanding of how it shapes reality", she will not be understood.[2] This illustrates how she has understood *education* as bringing together the *intelligent recognition* of paradox on the one hand and *empathic understanding* of how reality is shaped on the other. That deeply anchored view, which characterizes education could be studied and circumscribed as a novelty in the human sciences.

That novel theme is a complex issue in research and practices of the social sciences. In 1960 when Roberta Kevelson was talking to participants of an upcoming women movement in New England, she may not have been aware of the educational complexity that was implied in those conversations. For instance, when she later encountered A.J. Greimas' distinction between the surface structure and the deep structure of a text she became fully aware in how far that earlier work with the women in Falls River made issues from the genotext clear in her phenotextual conversations. The central question in context pertains to this type of activity, which remains partially in the dark: how and why do components of a text move from one level to another, and do they come backwards and forwards or do they move arbitrarily, and what is their relevance in the understanding of texts a social context? The only conclusion one could forward is that the dynamics of meaning and of meaning making within a text acquires specific points of orientation like those, which Greimas' nominations offer—is there not more to say?

It may be strange to consider those issues in the context of *education*. They can, however, have even more profound relevance of political and philosophical nature. Kevelson understood for instance in the course of her academic career, that hospitality to paradoxes, contradictions, open-ended statements and questions, expressions of chaos and disorder were at the level of her attitude as valuable as order, fixed dualities and the like. Her entire educational attitude as scholar and as teacher was determined by those outweighed values. She therefore practiced emancipation movements, new insights called semiotics, understanding and interpretation of legal texts in an anti-authoritarian manner.

One can often read the word 'dialogue' as an indication for this attitude. An example is given by Pencak, when she was asked in 1996 why she had studied

[1]Kevelson (1976), p. 29; Id.: (1987), pp. 18, 47, 194.

[2]Pencak (2002), (Op. Cit.), p. 4, and Pencak and Lindgren (1988), (Op. Cit.), p. 329f.

semiotics, believed in it and had been teaching it, saying: "… the greatest thing about semiotics is the recognition that we communicate not in a hierarchical fashion where an authority speaks downward but in a dialogic fashion among people who create a universe that is not finished, but open." At Penn State University, she won the AMOCO Award for Outstanding Teaching, an annually awarded prize out of thousands of Penn State Faculty Members. She had mentioned: "I am not there to give students anything. I am there to interact and get hem to know that the way we can interact is through an idea, which is something you hold on to at both ends." Pencak concludes that for her, teaching ought to be the creative exploration of ideas rather than the perfunctory presentation of accumulated wisdom."[3] But does one enter the field of a lawyer's self-understanding by means of this attitude combined with the new field filled with attention for signs and signification? That question is not in the first place a critical consideration but rather an invitation to grasp further and deeper meanings than an anti-authoritarian attitude can embrace—for instance to grasp the powerful inspiration to interpret *dialogue* not in terms of a *dyadic* relationship.

Kevelson had to fight the predominant opinion that semiotics is a specialization of the study of signs, whereby signs were understood as *things*, as basic *elements* of a discipline so that the art of fixing forms here a major method in a new garment. Her counter-argument was, of course, based upon the keyword 'dynamics'—but how is that to be understood in the case of this new discipline named 'legal semiotics'? It is of interest to remember that the basis for a well-understood social relation in the light of legal semiotics is *not* in any "I–Thou" or "Subject–Object" relationship, as was suggested in earlier attempts to create foundations for a social philosophy. No, (legal) *semiotics needs to study and reach out for new forms of inter-subjectivity*, as considerations of interaction and inter-activity in law and legal theory make clear. This need will be underlined in all cases in which the indefinable path from sign to signification becomes a truly human life-experience. That is the new insight she provoked without completely unfolding all its presuppositions and final effects in law and life. Kevelson was very near to this fascinating insight and its consequences, when she quoted already in her 1987 Peirce-study that she "took a radical stand against the traditional distinctions between methodology and logic", against false dichotomies of freedom v determinism, mind v body, change v discontinuity, and that what Peirce had said was correct: "*in reality, every fact is a relation*".[4]

Here is the true *nature* of semiotics: it is in the quality and essence of *relationships*—not in what we characterize as *signs* in an outer world of objects we constructed.

The necessity to initiate new research about the question whether 'signs' and even 'signification' can elucidate semiotics in specific discourses like law solely through predominantly philosophical research, seems evident. The hypothetical

---

[3]Pencak (2002), (Op. Cit.), pp. 333, 165ff.

[4]Kevelson (1987), (Op. Cit.), pp. 47, 194ff.

researcher will namely encounter the problem that 'signs' are not 'things', and 'things' do not remain 'things' when they are considered to be 'signs'. Because of this, a 'method' in the classical sense is not an appropriate instrument for semiotics. Methods withstand in a most evident manner the flow of life from sign to signification in which such event-characters like education find their place. Kevelson's tendency to interpret 'method' as equivalent to 'dynamic' seems in this context an inappropriate qualification. Further research into the possibilities to formulate a more appropriate concept for what in her vocabulary was called 'method' seems required.

4.2 Dialogue

It is remarkable that questions about the true understanding of semiotics lead us back to the Peircean observation that "everything can be(come) a sign"; the tricky issue is the every "*thing*" and its linguistic articulation. One should broaden Peirce's idea and become aware that "every*thing*" becoming a sign will because of that very becoming a sign no longer be a "thing". The no–*thing* is the challenging component of a relation and be aware that when it regards a *social* relation, it concerns most occasionally a human being. Semiotics brings a deeply engraved issue of everyday life to the fore. The language of our articulations pertaining to others as well as otherness *shapes* and more often *determines* the other human being and thus our relations to human life in general. The education activity has already emphasized this and Kevelson used for this the term *dialogue.*[5] The dialogue as a didactic device was her standard reference, and the narrative as dialogue her most widely embraced practice. She also reached with this term towards its implicit *holistic* approach, as Bakhtin, Buber and also Bohm had already brought to the fore. She wanted to reach out for semiotics as a multi-dimensional, multi-cultural, dynamic and contextual process of meaning making. Do not forget, that this is fundamentally a *social* process, in particular a way to shape daily life—imagined in above passages as 'walking the path from sign to signification'.

An implicit limitation is, that the expression 'dialogic' does *not* embrace this approach to semiotics, which indeed includes the search for an authentic relationship between man and man (as Buber proposed) determined by openness, loyalty and commitment. Her *Round Tables* were much in concordance with David Bohm's dialogue forms, focusing on small groups coming together for a few continuous days, avoiding tactical convincement and exposing own life experiences as the basis for knowledge and preparedness to create meaning. All these attempts to avoid authoritarian attitudes and to create forms of solidarity in view of knowledge

[5]The limitations of this use are a problem here. To express togetherness in linguistic terms is a major form of being together, as the multilingual and multicultural expression "I love you" illustrates. See: Sykes (2008), pp. 103f., 115.

and significance did *not* touch the deeper dimensions which determine human togetherness in forms of *interactivity* and *interaction* that support the traveler on the described path from sign to significance. Briefly worded in a short formula: *dialogue does not touch interaction.* The limitations of Kevelson's approach are concealed in this formula—which challenges further research into the *specific sociability created by semiotics.*

4.3 E-Education

If one keeps that short formula in mind, it appears old-fashioned to refer to the dialogue and to characterize the alternative of the authoritarian attitude as a dialogic attitude. To hypostasize "I" and "You" and treat them as fixated positions in patterns of speech acts will hardly be appreciated today. "Interaction" or "interactivity" is nowadays our central concept, and within a field of interactivity became *the ideal speech situation the ideal (social) norm.* That norm is mainly determined by a socio-technological mastering (social media participate powerfully) of ideologies, so that electronic communication occupies a most prominent place in all speech- and norm-performances. All this is absent in the arguments and explorations of Kevelson's attempts to promote the *legal semiotics* discipline.

Recent forms of electronic communication and forms of digital education have entered the field of the 'hearer' in the traditional 'speaker–hearer' relation and that is a revolution regarding the picture of such relations Kevelson had in mind. Electronic communication became furthermore a 'space' for human relationships of all kinds and measures, so that the connections between communication and legal practice changed law as well as legal subjects. A difference with earlier foundations of legal practice seems eye-catching: it is as if electronic communication has its wealth of techniques as a foundation for all structures of inter-human relations, so that remembrances of a dialogue appear senseless. This concealed change of foundational nature creates the suggestion that legal relations are solely based in interactivity—which also conceals a plea for pragmatism as the sole model for justice in social life. In classrooms and comparable educational spaces is the power of the multiple *apps* governing mind and behavior of the students a clear *sign* of this foundational situation. The *apps* impose a powerful guidance in the cases of educational growth as well as of the behaviors of subjects in law.

Actors in legal practices are continuously involved in processes of change; legal relations are thus relations between continuously changing subjects, and the speedy as well as often in-depth changes are never without smart phone images and related information. That field of change, inherent to what is called *interactivity,* seems a multidimensional field of communication in which law's semiotics should be met as a meaning making force. Law is never a matter of empowering fixated entities, but always a challenging invitation pertaining to changing participants. This perspective is inherent to the concept of legal semiotics, and appears in our days strongly related to the enormous diversity of electronic communication, of which the majority of *apps* and other instruments is in effect a matter of education. Legal semiotics should therefore assist lawyers in an important domain of their social profession: semiotics provides insight in facts and qualities of interacting entities because those entities change under the influence of their communication and its manifold techniques and programs. It should be research, in how far those e-communications contribute to better understand and perhaps solve problems with 'law as a system of signs' (Kevelson) on the one hand and social activities of the subjects of law on the other. *All interactions in law are performed by* CHANGING *actors: they change the law by means of their own activities of change*. Education in semiotic perspective is to induce change while changing, as recent forms of e-education illustrate. Or is it a form of inducing change *tout court*?

4.4 Law School Experiences

A last remark on the limits of Kevelson's semiotic approach pertains to the remarkable lack of engagement and experience with the specificities of Law School education. She was at Penn State University as well as the College of William and Mary engaged in philosophy departments and not in Law Schools, despite the fact that she developed and supported *legal* semiotics. This situation arises a number of exemplary questions, which we will only mention for the purpose of *future in-depth research*.

What opinion on law is inherent to her observation, that law—as the title of one of her most read books suggests—is a system of signs? If that is the case, what role fulfills the strong feeling for an anti–authoritarian attitude in this context, and what effect has her strong focus on legal theory in general? And what role has the *seminar* in contrast to *lectures* in a Law School's legal semiotics education?

Her Penn State Assistant and Colleague over many years, the historian William Pencak, reported: "While she was studying in various fields, prior to taking her doctorate, Bobbie had decided to create her own: legal semiotics. The inspiration for this idea came from a sentence in Thomas A. Sebeok's book *Contributions to the Doctrine of Signs*, which suggested that someone could do something with law and semiotics."[6] That story has been repeated in essays and conversations, but there are notes in her office papers, which tell otherwise. This could be a fruitful subject of further research, in particular to find the meaning of the words 'do something with law'. The 1988 book that is most known among lawyers, *The Law as a System of Signs* coordinates in an exemplary manner twenty-three essays with two specific features: with focus on the broad field within which law functions in modern society, including economics, politics, psychology and legal practice, and with focus on a deepening of Peircean concepts on that broad field. Peirce was known by philosophers and social scientists (far more than among lawyers and legal scientists)

[6]Pencak (2002), (Op. Cit.), p. 332.

for his drive to compare and combine powers of legal decision-making, wealth accumulation and political interests, no matter whether they regarded the activities of practitioners in the field or not.

Hence Kevelson's remark that semiotics "in law (and, by extension, economics and government) attempts to show the process of legal (or exchange or power-wielding) procedure as it develops in each case, and as the system of cases constitutes the moving parts of that moving and developing whole". And she adds that law embodies "Peirce's thought process made large, visible, mobile".[7] All in all, this is *not* a book for lawyers only! Legal scientists should moreover understand how the title did *not* proclaim that law was a system in the sense of any scientific systems theory and that signs were *not* defined in the sense of fixated particles of legal discourse, its theory and dogmatic included. The study should *orientate* the lawyer and *educate* him or her, but not *fixate* her or him professionally, because law is a discourse among discourses, and in the dynamics of those discourses is no place for fixation!

A fascinating and complex issue is basic for all considerations focusing on sign and signification in law: it is called *fiction*. Can fiction and system meet; is fiction for lawyers an acceptable concept? The question has at least two very different aspects in the framework of Kevelson's semiotics of law. The answer is complex: there is the '*grand level of law*' that plays a major role in Kevelson's legal semiotics. Here is fiction one of the powers to observe and to have been woven into the patterns of general events. She wrote in 1993: "It is we as semiotic investigators who weave and fabricate through our use of the method of semiotics the far side of this text we are calling Law".[8] In Courts and Cases, 'yarns are spun' and lawyers should be aware that laws, rights, human nature and the like are fabrications rather than natural, so that *fictions* are at this level the appropriate components of, and means to understand law. But things look different at '*the technical level of the law*' on which it is applied in accordance with the rules that create the internal structures of law. This level appears to be absent (spoken in general) in Kevelson's legal semiotics. But it is the technical/dogmatic level that makes law grow beyond borders and impregnates our mind.

This level embraces *fiction* as a keystone of its entire role in society. Already in 1908 was observed, how "it was probably a mathematician that first conceived the plan of feigning an unreality as a convenient step in the formation of an hypothesis, and then, having established his theory, conveniently let his fiction disappear. The law has been playing with such a fiction for centuries, in the course of which, the fiction, instead of disappearing, as it so conveniently does for the mathematician, has increased in girth and height, and has maintained its ghostly existence, in the face of the anathema of the philosopher and the fiat of the judicial decree."[9] The

[7]Kevelson (1988), (Op. Cit.), p. 223.
[8]Kevelson (1993), (Op. Cit.), p. 54.
[9]Deiser (1908), p. 131.

center of this fiction is *the legal person* and much of today's legal study and policy on the corporation is based on that fiction.

From this example is clear, in how far Kevelson's concern with law in her unfolding of legal semiotics pertains one-sidedly to the above mentioned *grand level of law*, and does not fit to the *technical level* what in Law Schools is taught: the techniques of applying and signifying legal concepts. The latter must be combined with legal education's molding a future lawyer's mind so that borderlines between fiction and reality, artificiality and naturalness are constantly surpassed in professional thought formation. Those formations dominate the form of social communication named *inter-activity*, which unfolds among participants in legal discourse and engages actors as well as audience.

While developing further research into the consequences of this two-level approach that characterizes Kevelson's legal semiotics, one should pay attention to the fact that the often-mentioned authoritarian attitude is not only inherent to human actors and their speech acts, but also to law's texts or discourses. This seems even a specific feature of a Law School education with 'legal semiotics' on its program. Students experience by means of that part of the program that to study law is never a solitary activity. Each fragment of that program requires training and skill formation in social behavior. The more difficult, complex and inaccessible the legal texts and cases in training are, the more profiled becomes the importance of the student's socialization. Here is the difference important between ex-cathedra education and seminar sessions. The first type of education requires from the student a careful listening to lectures and making notes of what has been said. The second requires a different attitude, including information, decision-making and discussion accompanied by non-individual reading and writing of texts. The latter will be *legal* texts, and create an awareness of the student pertaining to its professional character. The difference between 'artificial-' and 'natural language' texts—to mention this qualification in terms of linguistics—appears again to be a major issue in legal education!

It is in this context a remarkable fact, that Kevelson was mainly a reader of books on law without consulting even a few pages on legal education in connection with her desire to introduce semiotics in law's fields. It is even more remarkable and important in view of renewed research in the dimensions of *legal* semiotics, which stresses in how far law strives for equilibrated information about social norms and values, meanings and attitudes in a social pattern. Those elements and processes sustain the dynamics of life in society, Kevelson often underlined. Legal education contributes importantly to the realization of that goal. Law students discuss, create and check opinions, write and read, listen and decide. The major theme is the appropriation and execution of specific, most often professional, languages and linguistic articulations. Structures determining speech acts and texts bearing the qualification 'law' or 'legal' are the student's field. Only in that education context, relations between 'sign' and 'norm' will be studied, discussed and determined.

Analia Ayuso, a student in the 2009 *Roberta Kevelson Seminar on Law and Semiotics at Penn State University's Dickinson School of Law* wrote as a consequence of the above: "Since I am starting to think as a lawyer with the semiotics perspective, I understand that this change in the language of everyday life was one of the most important consequences … Lawyers have a powerful tool in their hands when they are applying the law in each case. I think that this power of the lawyers is incomplete without the knowledge of the multiple aspects of *meaning* of law."[10]

More than in average lectures, students experience their own presuppositions, their own attitudes resulting from authoritarian education behavior, and their own uses to manage meanings during a series of legal semiotic seminars. From the same 2009 seminar at Penn State, one reads a student reflecting upon the seminar: "Most of the time this class has felt like someone is speaking Chinese, a foreign language, in which I do not even know how to say 'hello'. The reason I believe that it has been so difficult is because it has been so engrained in our heads as law students to accept legal rules from case book readings and from professor's teaching that I have never looked beyond these rules for a more complex understanding of the law. Because law school to begin with is intimidating and foreign to most incoming students, it is hard for them to imagine yet another 'foreign language', an alternative way to look at law."

Indeed, to enter Law School, and more precisely: to participate in a Semiotics Seminar, is before everything else a form of 'average social behavior', which only part after part becomes questioned. The qualification 'normal' is authoritarian and therefore difficult to put into perspective. "Even in grade school, if a teacher tells you that this animal is a 'cat', then children believe the teacher and accept that animal as a cat without searching for more complex meanings. Even as we grow older, we conform to a lot of laws without knowing really what we are complying with. Citizens of a community do not speed through town because it is against the law. Few citizens ever look deeper into, for instance, *why* it is against the law. Citizens must conform or else face the punishment of a speeding ticket."[11]

Participating in semiotic considerations concerning such everyday life events is with necessity a loosening up the ties to authoritarian judgments, and thus for law a very special life experience. Pencak had registered words of Roberta Kevelson that should lead to the very same conclusion, for instance when she remarked: "What we take as law or a fixed judgment is always provisional. We are open to the world; the self is a dynamic sign in play that continually creates something genuinely new. Semiotics can keep freedom alive—it is experimental and anti-authoritarian; it is never under anyone's control; there are no masters or slave, only equals in relationships."[12]

These words fit to the reflections of Melina Zamora, when she writes in 2009 while confirming the context of this entire paragraph: "As students enter into American law schools they are bombarded with a different style of teaching than they have ever encountered in school before. The professor is the dictator and the student must give a correct answer to be saved from embarrassment in front of his

---

[10]Ayuso (2010), p. 13f.

[11]Zamora (2010), p. 21.

[12]Pencak (2002), (Op. Cit.), p. 144.

or her classmates. Traditionally, law students do not search for deeper meanings or reach for the foundation of the teachings of the professor, they simply accept the surface teachings of the professor."

And she positions the Semiotics Seminar in that it "focuses on trying to convince that semiotics can add value to our practice of the law. … I have come to realize that we as students of the law and even lawyers are already (and always will be) performing semiotic operations without even realizing it. The semiotics lawyers practice is just concealed or hidden in their own discourse they call 'law'. Lawyers give names and meaning to things such as cases, contracts, and court decisions. Collectively we call the management of these names and meanings 'legal practice'. The benefit of law students studying semiotics is in their being exposed to this way of looking at law to experience and enjoy its complexity. Finally, law accompanies semiotics in its endeavor to explore the cultural structures of life."

References

Ayuso AL (2010) Legal case and public awareness. In: Broekman JM, Pencak WA (eds) Signs of law: The Roberta Kevelson seminar in law and semiotics at Penn State University's Dickinson School of Law. Int J Semiot Law 23(1)

Deiser GF (1908) The Juristic Person (I). University of Pennsylvania Law Review and American Law Register 57(3), Vol 48 New Series

Kevelson Roberta (1976) Style, symbolic language structure, Syntactic change. Peter de Ridder, Lisse

Kevelson Roberta (1987) Charles Peirce's method of methods. John Benjamins, Amsterdam

Kevelson Roberta (1988) The law as a system of signs. Plenum Press, New York

Kevelson Roberta (1993) Peirce's aesthetics of freedom. Peter Lang, New York & Bern

Pencak W (2002) A conversation with Roberta Kevelson. In: Pencak W, Palecek C (eds) From Absurdity to Zen. The Wit and Wisdom of Roberta Kevelson, Peter Lang, New York

Pencak WA, Lindgren JR (1988) New approaches to semiotics and the human sciences. De Lang Publishers, New York etc.

Sykes G (2008) A short genealogy of realism: Peirce, Kevelson and Legal Semiotics. Int J Semiot Law 21(2)

Zamora MM (2010) A deeper understanding of law. In: Broekman JM, Pencak WA (eds) Signs of law: the Roberta Kevelson seminar in law and semiotics at Penn State University's Dickinson School of Law. Int J Semiot Law 23(1)

Chapter 5
Kevelson's Semiotics Today

Abstract A dynamic transition of language signs appears to be the key issue in the semiotic project. This is, as Kevelson suspected, particularly of essence in law and legal discourse. Semioticians thus determine the relations between *meaning* and *reality* so that we think to succeed to articulate 'how things really are'. Signs have for the lawyer legal quality because they reach him or her via legal discourse in his professional and social discourse. Legal signs are the result of a legal codification *before* a lawyer can unfold any legal activity. We thus consider the need to qualify (a) how signs become specifically legal, (b) whether there are parallel processes in other fields of professional signification, and (c) how the social field comes to accept those signs in their legal sense and evolves in accordance with the legal meanings of them.

Keywords Sign-translation · Attitude-change · Systems-theory · Articulation

5.1 Introduction

The stories of Melina and Bobby have much in common. They show the particular profile of Law School education by means of their striking contrasts as well as their reliance on common traits. In general, there is the limitation and often fixation of meaning making and meaning management. The latter characterizes law and its education, in contrast with the freedom of mind and interactivity in philosophy and politics, sometimes sustained by legal theoretical texts and (often) declarations of international law. It interests to note how semiotics plays a role in both.

Several remarks outline the profile and context of future research in Kevelson's legal semiotics. A most surprising discovery is, that students experience the semiotic dynamics clearer and more profoundly while participating in the Law & Semiotics Seminars than in their first contacts with traditional practices of directly applying the law. It would therefore be of interest to investigate the pattern of legal semiotics as it evolves *without* that pattern being embedded in the meaning

J.M. Broekman and F. Fleerackers, *Legal Signs Fascinate*, SpringerBriefs in Law,
https://doi.org/10.1007/978-3-319-69520-4_5

management of law's practices. Nobody has researched and provided a list of decisive differences between the story of Bobby and the remarks of Melina.

5.2 Two Stories

The two stories are about differences between a judgment of the constitutive qualities of law engendered by reflection and literature (Bobby) and on the other hand the qualities concluded by engaging into meaning policies in major legal practices like Courts or Law Offices, which are quoted and discussed as important in legal education (Melina). Those differences do not only pertain to the basic concepts of law, which intrinsically represent sign functions in view of a social order, but also to the general management of meaning in law's discourse in society. In other words: signs, which jurists receive from society's complex life, have for the lawyer legal quality because they reach him or her via legal discourse in his professional and later also social (mother tongue) discourse. Legal signs are thus the result of a legal codification before a lawyer can unfold any legal activity. But we have hitherto no concise semiotic theory about (a) how signs become specifically *legal*, (b) whether there are parallel processes in other fields of professional signification, and (c) how the social field comes to immediately, almost instinctively, accept those signs in their legal sense and evolves in accordance with the legal meanings of those signs. To prove the absence of such a theoretical foundation, consider a traffic light as a sign loaded with social and legal sign implications.

Wagner explained in her 2006 study on *The Rules of the Road* that road signage indeed "can be understood as a means, a mode of expression showing that legal culture is being communicated as expressed here: 'law is known by everybody'". Road signage shows what the consensus of the symbolic among the society is and how pervasive its message can be.[1] But her words also illustrate the absence of insight about the *dynamics* of signs at various levels of social communication and understanding, which includes specific forms of translation from signs to symbol to signification, as well as from code to word in the mind and the psychic capacity of the user of the road. The two stories fit perfectly into this consideration and the many ways semiotics are experienced in immediacy. How do such translations and their fixation of patterns of knowledge and behavior find place?

That problem of characterizing *translation* or *dynamic transition of language signs* appears to be the key issue in the semiotic project, and indeed, as Kevelson suspected, particularly of essence in law and legal discourse. It has above all its importance in all attempts of semioticians to determine the relations between *meaning* and *reality*. We most generally live in peace with the idea, that if we speak or conclude about a specific meaning, we then succeed to articulate 'how things

[1]Wagner (2006), p. 321.

really are'. The two above-mentioned stories have their most intimate commonness in this idea.

Is that idea reliable in semiotic respect? That question is a challenge and a powerful fascination: *has law to do with how things really are*? It seems completely *natural* when we articulate that question by means of applying methodologically: (a) the distinguishing of meaning and reality, and then (b) relating those two through a natural reference. This *naturalness,* which is common in both cosmic regions, is for Peirce as well as for Husserl a philosophical problem. Husserl can only develop a view on the above question in terms of a *non-naïve naturalness* because the question's presupposition is at distance to any 'natural-' or '*naïve naturalness*': a distance created by the reflexivity of the human mind, who distances itself from *meaning* and *reality* as *natural* concepts. The latter concepts are thus *non-natural.* How do they enter the field of semiotics of law? Has this question ever been considered? They are in any case the strong bond between the two stories and create a strong alertness about the true nature of conceptualization towards which those stories naïvely referred. Both illustrate the nature and consequences of *attitude change*; the latter seems crucial when social norms make us decide about the ultimate relationships that unite meaning and reality.

5.3 Semiotics Today

Many jurists who read about the Kevelson Round Tables two or more decades ago and think it belongs only to their life experiences, and the few legal scholars or practitioners who actually joined them in the US, Europe, Latin America or elsewhere may think that it is a precious fragment of their juridical experience in their past. No, to all of them is this Brief a message that past memories are extremely actualizing; they are a part of modern culture, a part of legal culture, a part of human law, a part of state practices and of human rights. Lawyers should notice this, even beyond their eventual tackling legal-semiotic issues.

Kevelson underlined the difference between thinking about *signs* on the one hand and exploring *semiotics* in a broad cultural context on the other. That became an important theme in the last decade of her activity and it only became more important in our post-modern days. Her remark could be the basis for *new research in the origins and effects of semiotics* in the 21st century. We may, in view of her remark, even consider this as a timely rebirth of our vital interest in law's theory by means of renewed research pertaining to its semiotic component.[2]

To combine law and semiotics is perhaps one of the most risky initiatives in social sciences and in philosophy in general. The first is often determined by the need to construct *fixed concepts* in order to understand and regulate the human

[2]A selection of RESEARCH THEMES on the basis of Kevelson's Works as well as her Office Papers and Notes is offered in Chap. 6, Appendix A.

world. The second is determined by an opposite: signs (which implicitly leads to significations that are themselves no more than new signs) do always lead us to *changes* of relations, views, lines of logic and understanding, to paradoxes signaling multiplicity and freedom. Pencak concluded: "Thus the life of the mind will remain alive, and flourish as a reinvigorated community of inquirers demonstrates the practical value of Peircean, Kevelsonian semiotics in creating a better world, aware of its freedom and unafraid to exercise it."[3] Here is the fruitful contrast: not the frozen concept of legal dogmas and theoretical constellations but a truly living law enables life—like semiotics does! Kevelson underlines this principle that binds law and semiotic forcefully. It was again Peirce who encouraged her to venture the formulation: *as soon as a sign becomes a fixed entity, it is no longer a sign*! Semioticians must therefore embrace the truly *dynamic* character of their attitude. Their very first concern should be, that *signs are events* and should only be understood as such.

It follows, that semiotics is not defined by a strict focus on equally strict defined of signs. That is neither the case in legal semiotics or in a general cultural and philosophical semiotics. The title of Kevelson's publication *The Law as a System of Signs* is in this regard treacherous: *signs* in law are *legal events* and their coherence is *legally* (and legal-institutionally) made into a system. *Legal* theory is not a *systems* theory. *Law* is not meant to be a *system.* Semiotics is the word that refers to the path from sign to signification—a path every one of us has to walk. On that path is no strict logic guiding us, but there is freedom and responsibility. Tyche rules over the dynamics of the walk and establishes ideas that create reality.

So, one should reconsider the ordinary meaning of words spoken to determine the meaning of 'semiotics', such as: "mind-blowing, radical, anti-authoritarian, and openness." Kevelson used them as the challenge of our days; those meanings could be the ground floor of further research in her ideas. In any case, we must conclude, those words are in her case challenging *law* beyond its boundaries. Is the combination *legal* and *semiotics* not only the expression to unfold a specific *theoretical* approach to law and legal discourse, but also (and perhaps in the first place) to find *openness, non-authoritarian views and practices, paradoxes to live with* in law?

This is not a *credo* but a call for further research, as this entire Brief is a plea and an outline for such research—not prescribed, but traceable. It provides for instance a new sense to the surprising and most enriching page of M. Robin entitled "76 Definitions of the Sign by C.S. Peirce".[4] It is in this context extremely interesting to encounter in this page *a plurality of contexts* for the notion of *sign* in the thoughts of Peirce. There is *no* mention of law or legal discourse among them, or any other indication of law's non-natural language in which a *sign* could function. This requires as a consequence a new in-depth search operation: what parallels, what contrasting or conforming meanings are mentioned, what could serve a lawyer's consideration pertaining to his or her professional attitude?

[3]Pencak and Palecek (2002), (Op. Cit.), p. 45f.

[4]www.perso.numericable.fr/robert.marty/semiotique/76defeng.htm, dd. 04.20.2017.

One more step is fruitful for this imagined future researcher: those circumscriptions should be compared to related research in various other fields in the human sciences: we suggest for instance M. Mead in cultural anthropology, E. Cassirer in philosophy of culture, Cl. Geertz in philosophy and anthropology of culture, N. Chomsky in linguistics, R. Jakobson and J. Kristeva in structuralism. Many more may follow. It is clear: legal semiotics places legal discourse in context.

But this is solely one of he many aspects concerned. There is a general reorientation once the study of semiotics is initiated, which reaches some of the most important foundations of 21th century philosophy. An example is in the difference as well concordance between semiotics and structuralism/post-structuralism. As was mentioned before, for instance the 'semiotic square'[5] representing semiotics and adapting to principles of structuralism introduced by A.L. Greimas, has been *en vogue* by lawyers and legal scholars But there is not one single study pertaining to the question how the various components *move* from one towards another. Often three of them are proposed as if they were empty boxes: the 'signified-interpretant' as Thirdness, the 'signifier-representamen' as Firstness and the 'referent' as Secondness. Those boxes are filled with terms having a foundational function (in particular a partly-representational function) of the legal case. Then the triangle can be doubled in the square of which each corner is filled with a determined opposition. Courts will construe the facts of the case so, that they fit within the semiotic triangle framework, so that finally the square appears to function as the relevant framework.

The case's architectonic structure is thus semiotically understood. A mark in the case materials is distinctive so that it serves as a 'source'. *Source* distinctiveness is the name for the extent to which the signifier in the case is distinctive of its signified. If there is little or no source distinctiveness, or if the signifier does not distinguish the signified, then the mark is generic. *Differential* distinctiveness describes the extent to which the mark's signifier is distinct from others in the case. This triangle–square technique is interestingly enough useful in many cases, for instance the various layers of trademark protection and the many cases in which that protection is legally questioned, as Garrett has shown in her 2010 essay. But the insight into 'creating the named places' and 'filling the places' in triangle and square does *not* bring any insight into the dynamics that are bringing the *case* as its *legal unfolding* to the fore—let alone the dynamics of legal semiotics. Exactly the same can be discovered in the above-mentioned relation between surface- and deep structure of a text. Dynamic essentials of semiotics would become clear, if there was any substantial research on the powers that bring genotextual elements of a legal text into the realm of the case's phenotext—and vice versa. Clarification of the dynamics involved in a semiotic approach to law does not seem to be achieved.

This is an astonishing conclusion after all the work Kevelson and others have done in view of changing the many faces of law by means of semiotic approaches. Does legal semiotics not consider the immense importance of a multi-dimensional approximation of signs? Wagner suggests in that regard to respect two axes of

---

[5]Clear examples of the square are for instance in: Harvill (2010), Garrett (2010), pp. 49–75.

reflection: (a) there is a 'mobility' between natural language and the professional non-natural languages in law as a discipline, which can only be understood in terms of dynamics. And (b) there is a specification concerning the meaning of terms employed in specialized languages, which focuses on dynamics. The contents of those latter terms are conform to a linguistic (semantic, lexical and textual) typology, a pragmatic (emitter, receiver, situations) and an environmental typology (marking, symbols, colors) typology, which is in essence also a matter of specified dynamics.[6]

The theme "Semiotics Today", so intensely represented and unfolded by Roberta Kevelson, requires a final remark. This remark is in the context of the challenging description of the final goal of developing a legal semiotics. She once said: "What we take as a law or a fixed judgment is always provisional. We are open to the world; the self is a dynamic sign in play that continually creates something genuinely new. Semiotics can keep freedom alive—it is experimental and anti-authoritarian; it is never under anyone's control; there are no masters or slaves, only equals in relationships."[7] But she was in the nineties of the last century already very worried about how people, philosophers and social scientists included, were treating semiotics, Pencak reports. Signs were treated as little peaces and like scavengers people did not make any effort to understand the true nature of semiotics. Opportunists took over, and used words like 'sign', 'signification' or even 'semiotics' itself as a buzzword to get their own narrative in the center of public interest. Those opportunists are still at work in the front lines of law, social sciences, ethics and other disciplines. They use 'semiotics' as a concept to further their own vision on life and in doing so disregard what Peirce had stated so many times: each sign is a sign itself only in context. One must remember what Peirce wrote already in 1873 about a *sign*: "A sign must in the first place have some qualities in itself which serve to distinguish it, a word must have a peculiar sound different from the sound of another word; but it makes no difference what the sound is, so long as it is something distinguishable. … As thought is itself a sign we may express this by saying that the sign must be interpreted as another sign." And in another context: "A sign is a thing which is the representative, or deputy, of another thing for the purpose of affecting a mind…"[8] Two Peirce quotations form decidedly one challenge: *to think* a *sign*: could it not be the most powerful definition of semiotics? That is indeed the case, when the *thinking* is performed properly. Unfolding semiotics, in particular in law and legal discourse, Kevelson has made clear, is always a matter of appropriate thought formation. And so is all research in that field.[9] We encountered three indications for such appropriateness; they help us to determine what it means to embark upon legal semiotics.

---

[6]Wagner (2010), p. 77f.

[7]Pencak (2002), (Op. Cit.), p. 144.

[8]See www.perso.numericable.fr/robert.marty/semiotique, (Op. Cit.), No. 5 (1873), No. 62 (non-dated text).

[9]Percy wrote in his 1983: "There is this perennial danger which besets semiotics: … with man using signs in everything that he does, semiotics runs the risk of being about everything and hence about nothing.", p. 85.

First, any plea for the statement "this is a sign" on itself, that is: without research concerning its context or without context *in se*, is nonsensical and would be characterized by Kevelson as the work of scavengers. A sign is a sign, and is solely relevant as a sign if a context lets it be a sign. That context determines semiotics as it determines the sign quality.

Second, 'finding' signs as belonging to a semiotic research is also nonsensical. There are no signs to find: there *are* only signs, and these are always on the path, on the move, engaged in their changes and further changing during the transition from sign to signification (which, as was said before, is able to become a sign in its turn).

Third, there is no unfolding of semiotics without and beyond a philosophical context. That context cannot be divided in fixed particles, like signs cannot, and cannot be brought into one dominant pattern called 'semiotic'. The latter is rather a togetherness of opinions, beliefs, values, ethical principles, religious rites and lifestyles, facts and fictions which can all come together in endless combinations into an ever changing entity we call 'context' at altogether different occasions.

Conclusion. An important conclusion of those three remarks is, that semiotic research, which is research into sign and signification, relies in the first place upon *articulation*. That reliance causes a general and rather unreflective tendency to consider semiotics as a matter of language (speech and writing) and in particular of linguistics (grammar, syntax, discourse). But *the complexity of articulation is a semiotic challenge in itself*. Those who study its lingual dimensions will encounter this complexity in the fact that *verbal* and *non-verbal* articulation appear of equal values and importance, so that these dimensions seem hardly beyond any measure of articulateness.[10] Those who study it historical or even archeological, experience the multiplicity of perspectives which (a) are extremely important for the intellectual and emotional background of the theme "semiotics today", (b) leads us to understand language as semiotically relevant, even if it is *separated from its linguistic articulation*—an attitude we seldom accept—and (c) brings archeological insights deep into our historical considerations.

The famous archeologist Bednarik stimulated the latter attitude, and his influence on modern semiotics should be studied as soon as one acknowledges the principle that there is no sign without context. Semiotics has thus taught us that "... the use of such sophisticated objects as beads and pendants in the Lower Palaeolithic demonstrates, beyond reasonable doubt, that *its hominids possessed well-established semiotic systems of various types*.[11] This evidence has so far hardly been considered, but has been neglected widely since its first tenuous mention 140 years ago. It is especially through this neglect, and through the frequent neglect of evidence not published in the English language, that the precarious models of recent

[10]Broekman (2017), (Op. Cit.), pp. 1–22.

[11]This has, next to Sebeok's zoo-semiotics, far reaching consequences. If all hominids create their own semiotic system, is the history of mankind in that perspective not identical to the history of semiotics?

years have been able to flourish as they did."[12] This is indeed, formulated from an unexpected angle, a most challenging question to semiotics today: will semiotics today also be appreciated as a "precarious model" (Kevelson's "scavenger's attitude") in social and historic-cultural sciences, or will it develop into a pillar of cultural and human sciences, which is particularly important for the social keystone called 'law'?

References

Bednarik RG (2000) Beads and the origins of symbolism. www.semioticon.com/frontline/bednarik.htm

Bednarik RG (2015) The tribology of cupules. Geol Mag 152(4), Cambridge

Broekman JM (2017) Verbal and non-verbal in Semiotics. In: SEMIOTICA. Journal of the International Association for Semiotic Studies/Revue de l'Association Internationale de Sémiotique, May 2017, No 126, p 19ff. De Gruyter Mouton

Garrett M (2010) Trademarks as a system of signs: a semiotic look at trademark law. Int J Semiot Law 23(1)

Harvill N (2010) Use the purpose by which all may benefit: the semiotics of 'Public Use'. Int J Semiot Law 23(1)

Pencak W (2002) A conversation with Roberta Kevelson. In: Pencak W, Palecek C (eds) From Absurdity to Zen. The Wit and Wisdom of Roberta Kevelson, Peter Lang, New York. In: Pencak WA, Lindgren JR (1988) New approaches to semiotics and the human sciences, De Lang Publishers, New York etc.

Percy W (1983) Lost in the cosmos. Picador USA, New York

Wagner A (2006) The rules of the road, a universal visual semiotics. Int J Semiot Law 19(3)

Wagner A (2010) Mapping legal semiotics. Int J Semiot Law 23(1)

---

[12] Bednarik (2000), Bednarik (2015), p. 758ff.

Part III
Appendices

This part offers *Two Appendices*: Appendix A is on the *notes, papers and other materials* that were in the office of Roberta Kevelson on November 28, 1998, the day of her death. Those papers are unpublished and not researched, so that this Appendix provides still virgin information. Appendix B is the most recent (2017), corrected and completed bibliography of Kevelson's *academic* publications since William Pencak's 1998 Appendix to his "Conversation with Roberta Kevelson".[1]

Reference

Pencak WA (1988) A conversation with Roberta Kevelson. In: Pencak WA, Lindgren JR (eds) New approaches to semiotics and the human sciences, essays in honor of Roberta Kevelson, De Lang, New York. p 329.

---

[1]Pencak (1988).

Chapter 6
Appendix A: The Roberta Kevelson Papers

6.1 Introduction

The boxes named "Roberta Kevelson Papers" contain the Office Notes and Papers of the late Distinguished Philosophy Professor Roberta Kevelson, Dr. Phil, Professor at Penn State University Berks Campus,

1. as packed in the office only a few days after her death in November 1998,
2. as transported to Texas Tech University (Institute for Studies in Pragmatism) in Lubbock, TX, USA, after that packing,
3. as rediscovered Sept/Oct 2012 in a public storage facility in Lubbock, TX, USA, and relocated in Nov 2012 at Penn State University.

6.2 Category Proposal

The relocation makes a provisory ordering of these Papers possible. They concern the following subjects, which all are in need of the (re)construction of a relevant context that clarifies their meaning and sense. Any publication of those notes and related texts is solely possible and meaningful after the completion of such contextual frames. At this moment have they been ordered in accordance to the following order.

6.2.1 Appendix B: Bibliographic Material

I. Texts, Notes, Miscellania.
II. Correspondence.
III. Round Tables.

J.M. Broekman and F. Fleerackers, *Legal Signs Fascinate*, SpringerBriefs in Law,
https://doi.org/10.1007/978-3-319-69520-4_6

History and historical descriptions, Correspondence, Participants + their bibliography, Texts, Publications (notes, and copies).
IV. US- And International Conferences.
Texts, Organization, Kevelson's Participation.
V. Peirce Studies
Photocopies, Notes, Drafts, Investigation of Kevelson's Peirce materials.

Two further remarks must be made in view of advanced research eventually taking place on those boxes:

(a) A general concern precedes the realization of research pertaining to the Kevelson publications: any appreciation of the multiple Kevelson publications does absolutely require as its basic reference instrument *a complete collection of the Kevelson book publications*—which could until now not be located in the US or the EU and seems not provided by any web site. An inventory of the boxes should not define the eventual content of such a complete collection.
(b) All boxes contain collected materials that correspond to the titles ordered in those groups. However, there are two groups that deserve particular attention. They are indicated as "Publications" and "On Ch.S. Peirce". The two are major components of Roberta Kevelson's own research and thus form basic materials for further scrutiny.

6.3 Bibliographical Materials

6.3.1 Article Publications

Many *article publications*, published and unpublished, typewritten and handwritten, function as a specific and often independent contribution to a book publication or other types of publications. Some have a single, others a double or plural use within a wider philosophical context.

One can only draw a final conclusion about the importance and function of those texts when a complete list of all article publications is made, and located in correspondence with the indexes of the book publications.

A decision about (re)publication of texts can only be made after this work is finished.

6.3.2 Complete Bibliography

A *complete bibliography* of the Roberta Kevelson works (see Chap. 6, Appendix B) can only be conceived on the basis of the foregoing activities, in particular those that are related to a clear order in the biographic materials. A most important line of demarcation is—as has been mentioned in the paragraphs of Chap. 3—the line between pre-academic and academic publications. These studies have in their turn to be expanded by a critical and comparative analysis of all publications present or mentioned in notes, diaries and other texts in the boxes. They should complete what is already known and published in books and web sites, including the many relevant sites on "legal semiotics", "Peirce studies" and "semiotics" in general, and form the basis for a complete collection of Kevelson book publications.

6.3.3 Charles S. Peirce

Kevelson's unique understanding and application of the philosophical insights of *Charles S. Peirce* should be recognized as one of the most important themes in the research on her work. The interdependence of this subject with all other components of Kevelson's work should be safeguarded.

One should from the very beginning order the many quotations of Peirce in Kevelson texts into two categories: those who have rhetorical-argumentative character and focus in essence wider (often legal-semiotic) themes, and those who belong to in-depth studies of the philosophy of Peirce, which are often also related to his semiotics. Relations with the rich supply of Peirce materials must be respectfully integrated in all research pertaining to Kevelson's work.

6.4 Publications

Several materials in the boxes suggest the need of a preliminary consideration to initiate *further publication* that pertains to several issues.

6.4.1 Charles S. Peirce and The Nation

A re-edition of the 4 volumes of Peirce texts contributed to "The Nation", from 1975 on, and published by Texas Tech University, Kenneth L. Ketner and James E. Cook (Eds) provided with a substantive context is suggested. The print proofs of the 1975 edition on the basis of which a new edition can be considered, are completely available in Box 28.

6.4.2 *Re-Editing the Peirce Bicentennial International Congress*

A new edition of the *Proceedings of the C.S. Peirce Bicentennial International Congress, 1981* should be studied. These Proceedings are no longer available and can easily be reprinted when using the complete print proofs available in Box 49. The 1981 publication by *Graduate Studies Texas Tech Univ. 23*, edited by K.L. Ketner, has not lost interest or relevance for Peirce studies and Kevelson explorations, so that a new edition should be feasible.

6.4.3 *Francis Lieber and Legal Hermeneutics*

A particular mention of studies on Francis Lieber in the context of early foundations of legal hermeneutics should be underlined. Kevelson has various publications and notes on that subject, and was convinced that a semiotic view of law's hermeneutics is extremely fruitful in view of theory and practices of law. The context fascinates: from 1856 until 1865, Lieber was professor of history and political science at Columbia University (then Columbia College). His title was chosen by himself, and made him the first officially designated political scientist in the United States. In 1860, he also became professor of political science in the law school, which post he held until his death. His inaugural address as professor at Columbia University (on "Individualism and Socialism or Communism") was published by the then College. He drafted legal guidelines for the Union army, the most famous being General Orders Number 100, or the 'Lieber Code' as it is now commonly known. The Lieber Code would form the basis of the first laws of war. An abridged version of the Code was published in *The War of the Rebellion: A Compilation of the Official Records of the Union and Confederate Armies* in 1899.

A conclusion is, that a Ph.D. Thesis on Kevelson's studies on Lieber as one of the earliest contributions to legal hermeneutics would be of unique and global interest, not only in the world of semiotics but also in the broader field of law's art of interpretation.

6.5 Research

Several research subjects are profiled when opening, ordering and exploring the boxes/papers. They are the main components of this Brief's ***call for a continuation of research***. Three of the most urgent subjects appear to be:

6.5.1 *Significs and Semiotics in Law*

The suggestion that Roberta Kevelson was the first (as she suggested more than once) to develop *legal semiotics*, although she had knowledge of Lady Welby's papers and thoughts and even the name of Jacob Israel de Haan in Amsterdam 1916 occupying the first chair in *legal significs*. Kevelson's view on semiotics in the phase of significs and the different philosophical background between signific an semiotics, in particular pertaining to law and legal discourse, is never researched.

6.5.2 *Semiotics of US and EU Jurisprudence*

Kevelson's appropriation of US- and European Jurisprudence should receive a profiled representation. There are many notes and indications in the boxes/papers who can support this research. A next step is to determine what influence her views and her extensive quotations on this field had on the development of legal semiotics in the 20th century.

6.5.3 *Charles S. Peirce*

Kevelson was famous for quoting Peirce. This most intimate relationship has hitherto never been researched, and nobody ever investigated (a) which quotations of Peirce in her books and articles were purely *illustrative*, and which were in fact *foundational* for her unfolding of the semiotics of law.

Insight in this matter would greatly profile the influence of Peirce in the field of legal semiotics—an often discussed but never precisely researched topic, which is doubtlessly worth a Ph.D. study or at least an essay in connection with an eventual re-edition of the 1981 Peirce Bicentennial Congress.

6.5.4 *Semiotics and Legal Education Today*

It has been explained in the above paragraphs that Roberta Kevelson had no experience with the particularities of Law School Education and Semiotics. Her many Round Tables did not take place in any legal education context and the number of students participating was extremely low. Her attitude in view of education in general was, however, in concordance wit the principles of Seminars and Round Tables as appropriate educational means, in particular in Law Schools. One concludes.

6.5.4.1. New research on the combination of the specificities of Law School Education in times of emphasis on legal practice and disinterest in legal theory is urgent.

6.5.4.2. The short history of Seminars and Round Tables in the context of Legal Semiotics should be reconstructed and the specific advantages of these education forms be evaluated in order to decide, in how far those experiences could contribute to today's programs of legal education.

6.5.4.3. The question has to be considered, whether the field of legal semiotics contains specific elements that are of particular importance for a lawyer's training—both in a practical and a theoretical sense. This calls (again) for a new judgment in view of semiotics contributing to the revaluation of US and EU Law School Programs.

Chapter 7
Appendix B: The Kevelson Bibliography

1976

Roberta Kevelson: *Introduction to the Logic of Questions and Answers*. Brown Working Papers 1; Brown University, Providence (Rhode Island), New York, 1976.

Roberta Kevelson: "Reversals and Recognitions: Peirce and Mukarovsky on the Art of Conversation", in: 19 *Semiotica, Journal of the International Association for Semiotic Studies/Revue de l'Association Internationale de Sémiotique*. De Gruyter Mouton. Berlin pp. 29–58.

Roberta Kevelson: *Style, Symbolic Language Structure, and Syntactic Change*. Series Semiotics of Language, No. 2, Peter de Ridder Press, Lisse, 1976.

1977

Roberta Kevelson: *Inlaws/Outlaws, a Semiotics of Systemic Interaction: "Robin Hood" and the "King's Law"*. Research Center for Language and Semiotic Studies, Indiana University, Bloomington, with Peter de Ridder Press, Lisse, 1977.

Roberta Kevelson: *Introduction to the Logic of Questions and Answers*, Brown Working Papers 2, Brown University, Providence (Rhode Island), New York, 1977.

Roberta Kevelson: *The Inverted Pyramid: An Introduction to a Semiotics of Media Language*, Research Center for Language and Semiotic Studies, Indiana University, Bloomington, with Peter de Ridder Press, Lisse, 1977.

Roberta Kevelson: "Language-Games as Systematic Metaphors", in: *Semiotica. Journal of the International Association for Semiotic Studies/Revue de l'Association Internationale de Sémiotique* 19, 1–2. De Gruyter Mouton. Berlin, 1977, pp. 29–58.

Roberta Kevelson: "A Restructure of Barthes' Readerly Text", in: 18 *Semiotica, Journal of the International Association for Semiotic Studies/Revue de l'Association Internationale de Sémiotique*. De Gruyter Mouton. Berlin, 1977, pp. 253–267.

J.M. Broekman and F. Fleerackers, *Legal Signs Fascinate*, SpringerBriefs in Law,
https://doi.org/10.1007/978-3-319-69520-4_7

1978

Roberta Kevelson: "Reversals and Recognitions, Peirce and Mukarovsky on the Art of Conversation", in: 19 *Semiotica, Journal of the International Association for Semiotic Studies/Revue de l'Association Internationale de Sémiotique*, De Gruyter Mouton. Berlin, 1978, pp. 29–58.

Roberta Kevelson: "Wittgenstein's Language Games as Systematic Metaphors", in; 19 *Semiotica. Journal of the International Association for Semiotic Studies/Revue de l'Association Internationale de Sémiotique*. De Gruyter Mouton. Berlin, 1978. pp. 281–320.

1979

Roberta Kevelson: "Relations of Nothings to Somethings: Functions of Sign Zero", in: II, 3 *Ars Semiotica* pp. 295–326, 1979.

1980

Roberta Kevelson: "Legal arguments as prototypes of discourse structure" in: *Semiotica. Journal of the International Association for Semiotic Studies/Revue de l'Association Internationale de Sémiotique*. De Gruyter Mouton. Berlin Vol. 32 No. 1 and 2, 1980.

1981

Roberta Kevelson: "Semiotics and the Art of Conversation", 32 *Semiotica. Journal of the International Association for Semiotic Studies/Revue de l'Association Internationale de Sémiotique*. De Gruyter Mouton. Berlin, 1981. pp. 53–80.

1982

Roberta Kevelson: "Comparative Legal Cultures", *American Journal of Semiotics*, Vol. 1. 1982, pp. 63–84.

Roberta Kevelson: "Legal Speech Acts: Decisions, Linguistics and the Professions" (R. Di Pietro Ed.) Abex Publishing, New Jersey, 1982, pp. 121–132.

Roberta Kevelson: "Peirce as Catalyst in Modern Legal Science: Consequences", in: 22 *Semiotica. Journal of the International Association for Semiotic Studies/Revue de l'Association Internationale de Sémiotique.* De Gruyter Mouton 1980 and M. Lenhart & M. Herzfeld (Eds.), Plenum Publishing Cie. New York, 1982.

Roberta Kevelson: "Peirce's Dialogism and Continuous Predicate", 18 *Transactions of the Charles S. Peirce Society*, Sheridan Press, Indiana, 1982, pp. 110–126.

Roberta Kevelson: "Semiotics and the Structures of Law", *Semiotica. Journal of the International Association for Semiotic Studies/Revue de l'Association Internationale de Sémiotique.* De Gruyter Mouton Vol. 35 No. 1 and 2, pp. 182–192, 1982.

1983

Roberta Kevelson: "Bridge Laws: Evaluative Review of Thomas A. Sebeok's 'The Sign and Its Masters'", in: *American Journal of Semiotics.* Vol. 2, 1983 pp. 84–108

Roberta Kevelson: “Francis Lieber and Legal Hermeneutics”, in: M. Lenhart & J. Deely (Eds.): *Semiotics 1981*, Plenum Press, New York, 1983.
Roberta Kevelson: “Peirce’s Method of Methods”, *International Congress on Logic, Methodology, and Philosophy of Science*, Abstracts, Salzburg, 1983.
Roberta Kevelson: “Methodological Solipsism: Charles S. Peirce’s Phenomenology” in: T. Winner et al. (Eds.): *Sign, Structure, and Function*. Mouton de Gruyter Publ. 1983, pp. 89–104.
Roberta Kevelson: “Charles Peirce’s Philosophy of Signs and Legal Hermeneutics”, *The 11th World Congress on Philosophy of Law and Social Philosophy*, Helsinki 1983. Publ.: Beiheft *Archiv für Rechts- und Sozialphilosophie*, Vol. 4 *IVR*. F. Steiner Verlag, Wiesbaden/Stuttgart, 1984.
Roberta Kevelson: “Time as Method in Charles S. Peirce”, *American Journal of Semiotics*. Vol. 2. No. 1 and 2. The Semiotic Society of America, (Publ.), 1983, pp. 267–276.

1984

Roberta Kevelson: “Peirce’s Speculative Rhetoric”, 17/1 *Philosophy and Rhetoric* (The Pennsylvania State University Press, (Publ.), State College, Pennsylvania) pp. 16–29, 1984.
Roberta Kevelson: “Riddles, Legal Reasoning, and Peirce’s Existential Graphs”, in: 57 *Semiotica. Journal of the International Association for Semiotic Studies/Revue de l’Association Internationale de Sémiotique*. De Gruyter Mouton Publishing pp. 197–223, 1984.
Roberta Kevelson: “Semiotics and Law”, in: T. Sebeok & J. Umiker-Sebeok (Eds): *Encyclopedic Dictionary of Semiotics*, De Gruyter Mouton Publishing, 1984.
Roberta Kevelson: “Semiotics in the United States”, in: T. Sebeok & J. Umiker-Sebeok (Eds): *The Semiotic Sphere*. Plenum Publishing New York, 1984, pp. 519–554.

1985

Roberta Kevelson: “Causation in Law: A Semiotics Perspective”, in: E. Landowski & D. Carzo (Eds.): Proceedings *Colloque International de Semiotique Juridique*, 1985.
Roberta Kevelson: “Economic Justice” in: 213 *Semiótica Jurídica* (Universidad Autonoma de Zacatecas, Mexico) pp. 95–109, 1985.
Roberta Kevelson: “Peirce’s Philosophy of Signs and Legal Hermeneutics”, in: E. Bulygin et al., (Eds.): *Man, Law and Forms of Life*. D. Reidel Publishing Cie. pp. 125–135, 1985.
Roberta Kevelson: “Toward a Global Perspective on Legal Semiotics”, in: D. Carzo & B.S. Jackson (Eds.): *Semiotics, Law and Social Science*, Liverpool Law Review & Gangemi Ed., pp. 81–93, 1985.

1986

Roberta Kevelson: “How’s of Why and Why’s of How”, in: *Proceedings of the Research Conference on Knowledge Seeking and Questioning*, in: 71 *Synthese*, 1986, pp. 91–106.

Roberta Kevelson: “Prolegomena to a Comparative Legal Semiotics”, in: J. Deely et al. (Eds.): *Frontiers in Semiotics*, Indiana University Press, Bloomington & Indiana, 1986, pp. 191–198.

Roberta Kevelson: “Property in Law and Semiotics”, in: S. Panou Ed., *Proceedings XII Congress of Philosophy of Law and Social Philosophy* IVR, F. Steiner Verlag, Stuttgart, 1986, pp. 125–136.

Roberta Kevelson: “Semiotics and Methods of Legal Inquiry”, in: 61 *Indiana Law Review*, Indianapolis, pp. 355–371, 1986.

Roberta Kevelson: “Toward a Global Perspective on Legal Semiotics”, in: B. Jackson & D. Carzo, (Eds.): *Semiotics, Law and Social Sciences.* 1986; also in: *Revue de Recherche Juridique: Droit Prospectif*, Aix/Marseille, Vol. 95, pp. 19–109, 1986.

Roberta Kevelson: “Growing, Discovering, and the Flow of Invention: Peirce and Kant”, in: G. Funke & T. Seebohm (Eds.), *Proceedings of the Sixth International Kant Congress*, University Press of America, Washington, 1986.

Roberta Kevelson: “Semiotics in the United States”, in: T.A. Sebeok & J. Umiker-Sebeok, (Eds.), *The Semiotic Sphere*. De Gruyter Mouton, Berlin, 1986, pp. 519–554.

Roberta Kevelson: “Law”, in: T. A. Sebeok (Ed.) *Encyclopedic Dictionary of Semiotics*, De Gruyter Mouton, Berlin, 1986, pp. 438–443.

1987

Roberta Kevelson, Ed.: “*Law and Semiotics I*”. Round Table on Law and Semiotics. Plenum Press, New York & London, 1987.

Roberta Kevelson: “Introduction to the First Round Table on Law and Semiotics”, in: Roberta Kevelson, (Ed.): *Law and Semiotics I.* Round Table on Law and Semiotics. Plenum Press, New York & London, 1987. pp. 1–24.

Roberta Kevelson: “Repugnancy and Paradox in Law: A Peircean Point of View”, in: Roberta Kevelson (Ed.): *Law and Semiotics I* Round Table on Law and Semiotics. Plenum Press, New York & London, 1987.

Roberta Kevelson: *Charles S. Peirce’s Method of Methods*, John Benjamin’s Publishing, Amsterdam, 1987.

Roberta Kevelson: “Representation in Law”, in: H. Georg (Ed.): *Recherches Semiotiques/Semiotic Inquiry*. Van den Hoeck & Ruprecht, Göttingen, 1987.

Roberta Kevelson: “Review of the Round Table on Law and Semiotics”, in: T. Sebeok & J. Umiker-Sebeok (Eds): *The Semiotic Web*, De Gruyter Mouton Berlin, 1987.

1988

Roberta Kevelson: *The Law as a System of Signs*, Plenum Press, New York & London, 1988.

Roberta Kevelson, (Ed.): *Law and Semiotics II*. Round Table on Law and Semiotics, Plenum Press, New York & London, 1988.

Roberta Kevelson: “Introduction to the Second Round Table on Law and Semiotics”, in: Roberta Kevelson (Ed.): *Law and Semiotics II*. Round Table on Law and Semiotics, Plenum Press, New York & London, 1988, pp. 1–12.

Roberta Kevelson, "The New Realism and Lawlessness in Kaleidoscope", in: Roberta Kevelson (Ed.): *Law and Semiotics II.* Round Table on Law and Semiotics, Plenum Press, New York & London, 1988.
Roberta Kevelson: "Peirce's Studies on the Science of Value", in: A. Mandelker et al., (Eds.): *(Festschrift for Thomas G. Winner) Canadian-American Slavic Studies*, Vol. 22, Issue 4, pp. 57–75, Brill, 1988.

1989
Roberta Kevelson, (Ed.): *Law and Semiotics III.* Round Table on Law and Semiotics, Plenum Press, New York & London, 1989.
Roberta Kevelson: "Property: The Legal Thing as Artwork" in: Roberta Kevelson (Ed.): *Law and Semiotics III.* Round Table on Law and Semiotics, Plenum Press, New York & London, 1989. Reprint in: Jan M. Broekman & Larry C. Backer: *Signs in Law—A Source Book.* Springer, 2015, p. 213ff.
Roberta Kevelson: "Pragmatic Method and Some Consequences", in: Roberta Kevelson, (Ed.): *Law and Semiotics III.* Round Table on Law and Semiotics, Plenum Press, New York & London, 1989.
Roberta Kevelson: "Sinister Intent, Political Fallacy, and the Pearlizing of Value in Law" in: V. Ferrari & C. Faralli (Eds.), *Laws and Rights.* Dott. A, Guiffre Editions, Milano, 1989, pp. 593–610.

1990
Roberta Kevelson: "Law and Semiotics" in: Walter A. Koch (Ed.): *Semiotics in the Individual Sciences*, Brockmeyer Verlag, Bochum, 1990, pp. 282–298.
Roberta Kevelson: *Peirce, Paradox, Praxis. The Image, The Conflict, The Law.* Mouton de Gruyter, Berlin, New York 1990.
Roberta Kevelson: "Semiotics as Exploratory: Peirce's Art of the Possible", in: J. Delledalle (Ed.), *Proceedings IASS 1989*, De Gruyter Mouton, Berlin 1990, pp. 1333–1341.
Roberta Kevelson: "Tom Paine: Rights and Revolutions", *International Journal for the Semiotics of Law*, Kluwer Academic Publishers, Dordrecht, 1990, pp. 169–186.
Roberta Kevelson: "Transactions and the Increase of Goods and Meaning: A Semiotics Approach", in: 41 *Syracuse Law Review*, Special issue: *Law and Economics*, Syracuse University, New York, 1990, pp. 7–25.

1991
Roberta Kevelson, (Ed.): *Action and Agency. Fourth Round Table on Law and Semiotics*, Peter Lang Publishing, New York/Bern, 1991.
Roberta Kevelson: "Legal Agency As Facsimile and Iconic Function: Authority, Power, Representation" in: Roberta Kevelson, (Ed.): *Action and Agency. Fourth Round Table on Law and Semiotics*, Peter Lang Publishing, New York/Bern, 1991, pp. 135–156.
Roberta Kevelson: Transfer, Transaction, Asymmetry: Junctures Between Law and Economics from the Fish-Eye Lens of Semiotics" in: *Syracuse Law Review*, Vol. 42, No. 7, Syracuse University, New York, 1991.

Roberta Kevelson: "The Confusion of Language in Legal Thought", in: Hans Joachim Koch & Ulfried Neumann (Eds.), Archiv für Rechts- und Sozial-Philosophie/IVR, Franz Steiner Verlag Wiesbaden, Stuttgart, 1991.
Roberta Kevelson, (Ed.): *Peirce and Law: Issues in Pragmatism, Legal Realism, and Semiotics*, Peter Lang Publishing, New York/Bern, 1991.
Roberta Kevelson: "Charles S. Peirce", in: Roberta Kevelson, (Ed.): *Peirce and Law: Issues in Pragmatism, Legal Realism, and Semiotics*, Peter Lang Publishing, New York/Bern, 1991.
Roberta Kevelson: "Peirce and Community: Public Opinion and the Legitimization of Value in Law", in: Roberta Kevelson, (Ed.): *Peirce and Law: Issues in Pragmatism, Legal Realism and Semiotics*, Peter Lang Publishing, 1991.

1992
Roberta Kevelson (Ed.): *Law and Aesthetics*, Peter Lang Publishing, New York/Bern, 1992.
Roberta Kevelson: "The Art of Discovery in Law", in: Roberta Kevelson, (Ed.): *Law and Aesthetics*, Peter Lang, New York/Bern, 1992.
Roberta Kevelson, (Ed.): *Law and the Human Sciences Series.* Peter Lang, New York/Bern, 1992.
Roberta Kevelson, (Ed.): *Law and the Human Sciences. Fifth Round Table on Law and Semiotics.* Peter Lang Publishing, New York/Bern, 1992.
Roberta Kevelson: "Pragmatism, Utopic Constructions, Legal Myths", in: Roberta Kevelson (Ed.), *Law and the Human Sciences.* Fifth Round Table on Law and Semiotics, Peter Lang Publishing, New York, Bern, 1992, pp. 193–218.
Roberta Kevelson: "Property as Rhetoric in Law", in: *Cardozo Studies in Law & Literature*, Vol. 4, New York, 1992, pp. 189–206.

1993
Roberta Kevelson, (Ed.): *Flux, Complexity, and Illusion.* Sixth Round Table on Law and Semiotics, Peter Lang Publishing, New York, Bern, 1993.
Roberta Kevelson: "Aspects of Property in Law: The Cultural, the Incorporated, the Intellectual, the New.", in: Roberta Kevelson (Ed.), *Flux, Complexity, and Illusion.* Sixth Round Table on Law and Semiotics, Peter Lang Publishing. New York/Bern, 1993.
Roberta Kevelson: "A Peircean Approach to Human Rights", *International Journal for the Semiotics of Law*, Vol. 6, No. 1. Kluwer Academic Publishers, Dordrecht, 1993. pp. 71–88.
Roberta Kevelson: *Peirce's Aesthetics of Freedom: Possibility, Complexity, and Emergent Value* Peter Lang Publishing, New York/Bern, 1993.
Roberta Kevelson: "Public Opinion and Human Rights", in: P. Ahonen, (Ed.), *Tracing the Semiotic Boundaries of Politics*, Indiana Univ. Press, Indianopolis, 1993, pp. 159–174.
Roberta Kevelson, (Ed.): *Codes and Customs: Millennial Perspectives*. Series: *Critic of Institutions*, Peter Lang Publishing, New York/Bern, 1994.

Roberta Kevelson: "Peirce at the Millennium", in: Roberta Kevelson (Ed.), *Codes and Customs: Millennial Perspectives*. Peter Lang Publishing, New York/Bern, 1994, pp. 153–176.

1994

Roberta Kevelson, Ed.: *The Eyes of Justice. Seventh Round Table on Law and Semiotics*; Semiotics and the Human Sciences Series, Peter Lang Publishing, New York/Bern, 1994.
Roberta Kevelson: "Zero Sign and the Science of Justice", in: Roberta Kevelson (Ed.): *The Eyes of Justice*. Seventh Round Table on Law and Semiotics, Peter Lang Publishing, New York/Bern, 1994, pp. 139–158.
Roberta Kevelson: "Lex Talionis", *International Journal for the Semiotics of Law*, Vol. 7, No. 2. Kluwer Academic Publishers, Dordrecht, 1994. pp. 155–170.

1995

Roberta Kevelson, Ed.: *Conscience, Consensus, & Crossroads in the Law: Eighth Round Table on Law and Semiotics*, Peter Lang Publishing, New York/Bern, 1995.
Roberta Kevelson: "Boyle's Lock'N' Key: Consent and Contrast", in: Roberta Kevelson (Ed.): *Conscience, Consensus, Crossroads in the Law*, Eighth Round Table on Law and Semiotics, Peter Lang Publishing, New York/Bern, 1995, pp. 163–180.
Roberta Kevelson: "Crisis in International Law", in: E. Pattaro (Ed.): IVR Proceedings: *Challenges to Law at the End of the 20th Century*, Milano, 1995.
Roberta Kevelson: "Icons of Justice/Spirit of Laws" in: *International Journal for the Semiotics of Law*, Vol. 8, No. 3. Kluwer Academic Publishers, Dordrecht pp. 227–239, 1995.
Roberta Kevelson (Ed.): *Spaces and Significations*. Peter Lang Publishing, New York/Bern, 1995.
Roberta Kevelson: "Law at the Border", in: Roberta Kevelson (Ed.): *Spaces and Significations*, Peter Lang Publishing, New York/Bern, 1995.

1996

Roberta Kevelson, (Ed.): *Peirce, Science, Signs*. Series Semiotics and the Human Sciences (Peter Lang Publishing, New York/Bern, 1995.
Roberta Kevelson: "Eco and Dramatology", in: R. Capozzi (Ed.), *Reading Eco*. Indiana University Press, Indianapolis, 1996.
Roberta Kevelson: "Justice as Artifice and Sign", in: ARSP: Archiv für Rechts- und Sozial-Philosophie: *Law, Justice, and the State*. Franz Steiner Verlag Wiesbaden, Stuttgart, 1996.
Roberta Kevelson, (Ed.): *Law and the Conflict of Ideologies; Ninth Round Table of Law and Semiotics* (Peter Lang Publishing, New York etc. 1996).
Roberta Kevelson: "Knotmaking in the Law: Semiotic Perspective on Ideological Conflict" in: Roberta Kevelson (Ed.), *Law and the Conflict of Ideologies*. Ninth Round Table of Law and Semiotics, Peter Lang Publishing, New York/Bern, 1996, pp. 105–116.

1997

Roberta Kevelson & John Brigham (Eds): *States, Citizens, Questions of Significance. Tenth Round Table of Law and Semiotics*, Peter Lang Publishing, New York, 1997.

Roberta Kevelson: "Immigrants and the New Anarchism: On Displaced Values", in: Roberta Kevelson & John Brigham (Eds): *States, Citizens, Questions of Significance.* Tenth Round Table of Law and Semiotics, Peter Lang Publishing, New York, 1997.

1998

Roberta Kevelson, (Ed.): *Hi-Fives: A Trip to Semiotics.* Peter Lang Publishing, New York, 1998.

Roberta Kevelson: "When Old is New Again" in Roberta Kevelson, (Ed.): *Hi-Fives: A Trip to Semiotics.* Peter Lang Publishing, New York, 1998, pp. 1–13.

Roberta Kevelson: "Semiotics in a Peircean Light" in: Roberta Kevelson, (Ed.): *Hi-Fives: A Trip to Semiotics.* Peter Lang Publishing, New York, 1998, pp. 57–71.

Roberta Kevelson: "Peirce's Semiotics as Complex Inquiry: Conflicting Methods", in: Jacek Juliusz Jadacki & Witold Strawinski (Eds): *In the World of Signs: Essays in Honor of Professor Jerzy Pelc*, Rodopi, Amsterdam, 1998.

Roberta Kevelson & Joel Levin (Eds): *Revolutions, Institutions, Law: Eleventh Round Table on Law and Semiotics.* Peter Lang Publishing, New York, 1998.

William Pencak & Ralph J. Lindgren, (Eds): *New Approaches to Semiotics and the Human Sciences: Essays in Honor of Roberta Kevelson.* Peter Lang Publishing, New York, 1998.

1999

Roberta Kevelson: *Peirce and the Mark of the Gryphon.* St. Martin's Press, New York, 1999.

Roberta Kevelson: *Peirce's Pragmatism*, Peter Lang Publishing, New York, 1999.

Roberta Kevelson: "Semiotic Philosophy of Law" in: Christopher Berry Gray, (Ed.): *The Philosophy of law. An Encyclopedia.* Vol II Garland Publishing, Inc., New York/London 1999, pp. 792–794.

Roberta Kevelson: "Peirce, Charles Sanders (1839–1914)" in: Christopher Berry Gray, (Ed.): *The Philosophy of law. An Encyclopedia.* Vol II, Garland Publishing, Inc., New York/London, 1999, pp. 635–637.

FSC
www.fsc.org
MIX
Papier | Fördert
gute Waldnutzung
FSC® C083411

Kolibri 360 GmbH
Ferdinand-Jühlke-Straße 7
99095 Erfurt, Deutschland
produktsicherheit@kolibri360.de